No Free Lunch—Pay Back Welfare!!!

A unique idea to provide a great US safety-net and put taxpayers first.

President Bush and President Obama both agreed that a database of health records needed to be established on behalf of the people. It is a good idea. There needs to be a record of each citizen in the United States so that it will be much easier to get a full picture of a patient in any medical provider setting from doctor's offices, laboratories, imaging, and other specialties. Dollars owed by all can also be kept in the database.

Most Americans are aware of the major battle on health insurance and healthcare "reform" as in Obamacare, after seven years, continues in the Halls of Congress. A Democratic Congress and the former POTUS decided by themselves to spend a trillion dollars on a government take-over of healthcare in 2010. They knew it would possibly improve the lives of just 17% of the people and seven years later the number has not been achieved as just 10 million in total are signed up. Obamacare usage is so insignificant, it should be on nobody's agenda.

When the bill passed, Congress willfully disrupted the lives of the other 83% of Americans by providing them with less healthcare, less medical provider choices, huge deductibles, and more taxes. You cannot take $700 billion from Medicare for Obamacare and make Medicare better. It is insane. Perhaps Senior Citizens will have to find employment again to buy back what was stolen by government without their permission?

Obamacare's big users get big welfare subsidies to afford it or nobody would be enrolled. The big winners of course are trial lawyers and the big insurance companies while the people have been left holding the bag, healthcare has become the biggest welfare expense. In this book, we introduce the notion that all welfare should be paid back. We show both sides of the welfare story and offer some unique thoughts about how welfare can become an item that is paid back when people are doing well.

There is no free lunch and this book shows the technology solutions that can help the US help you avoid having to pick up the tab. We enjoy describing how to account for any freeloader who takes from the system. What happens today if somebody on welfare for 50 years wins a couple hundred million on the Powerball? You bet, we solve that problem. It's in here.

LETS GO PUBLISH

I0040054

BRIAN W. KELLY

Copyright © 2017, 2018 Brian W. Kelly   Editor, Brian P. Kelly
Author Brian W. Kelly

No Free Lunch—Pay Back Welfare!!
A unique idea to provide a great safety-net and put taxpayers first.

Disclaimer: Though judicious care was taken throughout the writing and the publication of this work that the information contained herein is accurate, there is no expressed or implied warranty that all information in this book is 100% correct. Therefore, neither LETS GO PUBLISH, nor the author accepts liability for any use of this work.

Trademarks: A number of products and names referenced in this book are trade names and trademarks of their respective companies.

Referenced Material: *The information in this book has been obtained through personal and third-party observations, interviews, and copious research. Where unique information has been provided or extracted from other sources, those sources are acknowledged within the text of the book itself or at the end of the chapter in the Sources Section. Thus, there are no formal footnotes nor is there a bibliography section. Any picture that does not have a source was taken from various sites on the Internet with no credit attached. If resource owners would like credit in the next printing, please email publisher.*

Published by: .... LETS GO PUBLISH!
....
Publisher: .... Brian P. Kelly
....
Editor: Brian P. Kelly
Mail Location: .... P.O. Box 621, Wilkes-Barre, PA 18703
Web site...www.letsgopublish.com

Library of Congress Copyright Information Pending
Book Cover Design by Brian W. Kelly;
Original Editing by Melissa L. Sabol

ISBN Information: The International Standard Book Number (ISBN) is a unique, machine-readable identification number, which marks any book unmistakably. The ISBN is the clear standard in the book industry. 159 countries and territories are officially ISBN members. The Official ISBN For this book is on the outside cover:
978-1-947402-24-9

The price for this work is :   **$9.95USD**

10	9	8	7	6	5	4	3	2	1

Release Date: February 2017, January 2008

LETS GO PUBLISH!

Dedication

*I dedicate this book in is new incarnation
To the magnificent McKeown Girls
Who, while beautiful among all beauties in their outward
appearances possess an inward beauty that separates these
ladies from the rest.*

*They are the daughters of Nick and Emma McKeown. Along
with their very remarkable husbands, I list them in order of
birth: Kathleen and Angel Dave Conklin, Rita and Frank
DeRiancho, Joan and Tommie Nelson. The Jersey Tomato
could not make it to the picture shoot. You can't even imagine
how high on the kindness scale these people operate. They are
also wonderful first cousins and avid supporters of all of my
writing efforts.*

*My wife, my whole family, my brothers and sisters, and all of
our other wonderful cousins and all the friends you have
touched are tickled to know and be known by the inimitable
McKeown Ladies.*

Thank You and the Best!

Acknowledgments

I would like to thank many, many people for helping me in this effort.

I appreciate all the help that I have received in putting this book together as well as all of my other 136 published books.

My printed acknowledgments had become so large that book readers "complained" about going through too many pages to get to page one of the text.

And, so to permit me more flexibility, I put my acknowledgment list online, and it continues to grow. Believe it or not, it once cost about a dollar more to print each book.

Thank you and God bless you all for your help.

Please check out www.letsgopublish.com to read the latest version of my heartfelt acknowledgments updated for this book. Click the bottom of the Main menu!

To sum up my acknowledgments, as I do in every book that I have written, I am compelled to offer that I am truly convinced that "the only thing you can do alone in life is fail." Thanks to my family, good friends, Wily Ky Eyely and a wonderful helping team, I was not and continue to be --- not alone.

Table of Contents

Dedication v

Acknowledgments... vii

Table of Contents ix

Preface:.. xi

About the Author............................ xvii

Chapter 1 Should Welfare Be Paid Back?.................................... 1

Chapter 2 Welfare Debate Among Americans............................. 11

Chapter 3 Americans Do Not Always Agree 19

Chapter 4 Freedom From Government?...................................... 29

Chapter 5 Emergency Care via EMTALA 37

Chapter 6 Other Medical Insurances 51

Chapter 7 Accountability 59

Chapter 8 Personal Accountability System—Phased Implementation..... 71

Chapter 9 Welfare Accountability... .. 81

Chapter 10 Summary & Conclusions 89

Other books by Brian Kelly: (Amazon.com, and Kindle)...................... .. 96

Preface:

How about a free lunch? The US government gives millions of lunches away every day in one way or another. Did you get one today?

When I updated this original 2008 book about then current, domestic, political and constitutional issues intertwining with public consciousness, I became immersed, once again, in that vortex of all-too-familiar concerns about our government. I was compelled to add a few paragraphs about the Obama presidency considering the transparent failures of the coronated administration.

As I undertook the task of updating, I became so smothered in the existential issues that had since developed that I was pushed to delve further into the examination of the underlying issues. Thus, the project moved beyond what one may consider to be a standard update/ revision to the point that, when I received the book back from the editor, I noticed that she had split the original book not once but twice and had created two additional, entirely distinct books.

An update to the first book, *Obama's Seven Deadly Sins*, was released concurrently with the predecessor of this book in summer 2016. It advises that the deadliest sin of all is indeed Obama's approach to healthcare, or what many now call Obamacare. This book's predecessor, *Healthcare and Welfare Accountability* was already within Obama's Seven Deadly Sins as a chapter and when split, it was first released as *Healthcare Accountability*.

In summer 2016, in the middle of the Trump presidential campaign, I modified it to reflect how a future Trump presidency might view such accountability. Here I am again with President Trump at the helm of the Big Ship US. Now we examine what President Trump should consider doing in the area of accountability. I make some very strong recommendations.

The Editor noted that the book offered a coherent, common sense solution to the biggest problem with US healthcare for all -- its huge cost. It happens that the much of the same overall solution can be applied to the current high-cost US welfare system, the theme of this book.

She suggested that it be released as its own separate offering and that's what I originally did but now we are at round three. The original book, *Healthcare Accountability* offers a unique and compelling solution to the problem of healthcare cost. It is still available on Amazon & Kindle.

Those following the healthcare debate note that President Bush and President Obama both agreed that a database of health records needed to be established on behalf of the people. It is a good idea. There needs to be a record of each citizen in the United States so that it will be much easier to get a full picture of a patient in any medical provider setting from doctor's offices, laboratories, imaging, and other specialties.

Most Americans are aware of the major battle on health insurance and healthcare "reform" as in Obamacare, which after seven years, continues in the Halls of Congress even today. A Democratic Congress and the former POTUS decided by themselves to spend a trillion dollars on a government take-over of healthcare in 2010.

They knew it would possibly improve the lives of just 17% of the people and seven years later the number has not been achieved as just 10 million in total are signed up for Obamacare. Obamacare is so insignificant, it should be on nobody's agenda.

When the bill passed, Congress willfully disrupted the lives of the other 83% of Americans by providing them with less healthcare, less medical provider choices, huge deductibles, and more taxes. You cannot take $500 billion from Medicare for Obamacare and make Medicare better. It is insane. Perhaps Senior Citizens will have to find employment again to buy back what was stolen by government without their permission?

Obamacare's big users get big subsidies to afford it or nobody would be enrolled. The big winners of course are trial lawyers and the big insurance companies while the people have been left holding the bag. Healthcare is the biggest welfare expense. In this book, we introduce the notion that all welfare be paid back. We show both sides of the welfare story and offer some unique thoughts about how welfare can become an item that is paid back when people ae doing well.

There is no free lunch and this book shows the technology solutions that can help you avoid having to pick up the tab. We enjoy describing how to account for any freeloader who takes from the system. What happens today if somebody on welfare for 50 years wins a couple hundred million on the Powerball? You bet, we solve that problem. It's in here.

Logic dictates that you cannot take $500+ billion from Medicare to make it better. Will Senior Citizens have to find employment again to buy back what they gave up to Obamacare?

The big winners, in this scenario, were the trial lawyers and the big insurance companies. The people (as in We the People) were left holding the bag. In this accountability book, we describe, in reasonable detail and in words that any American can understand how to make the healthcare system -- both ER and Medicaid, and the remnants of Obamacare more accountable to the people.

There is no free lunch and, in order to gain accountability in welfare and healthcare, we must begin to keep track of things. May I repeat that President Bush and President Obama both agreed that a database of citizen health records needed to be compiled and it is, indeed, a very good idea. When President Trump slogs through all of his early to-dos, we can bet that he too will agree that a database of electronic health records for citizens is a great idea and we need to make it work. I suspect he will also be impressed with a Personal Accountability System that keeps track of everything Americans have given to other Americans from the time this system began.

In such a system, there would be health records and payback-accountability records for each citizen in the United States. In this way, it would be much easier to get a full picture of a patient in any medical provider's setting. It would also help us all know who owes what back to Uncle Sam and the people. You go in, give your cards, and poof, the provider you have never met has your permanent medical record known as an Electronic Health Record.

This book provides a logical and clear blueprint that defines the terms for organization of online database records and discusses the entities that are positioned to "own" your health data. It also offers suggestions specifying which entity would be the proper custodian of such vital data. Hint—not government or insurance companies.

This book on accountability identifies the best means of managing the collection of health records in a "system in the sky." Additionally, the book helps Americans understand the issue and gives a solution that assures privacy and locks out the bad guys who want your health data so badly they can taste it. As a bonus, it offers a cogent solution for welfare accountability.

Why did Brian W. Kelly write this book?

Brian W. Kelly wrote this book because he cares, and I am publishing this book because I care. This book points out many of the issues and makes a case for patient accountability and then shows how it can be achieved. It identifies the best means of managing the collection of health records in a "system in the sky."

Additionally, it will help you understand the issue and give you a solution that assures your privacy and locks out the bad guys who want your health data so bad they can taste it. As a bonus, it offers a cogent solution for welfare accountability. President Trump would do well to have his team evaluate this book for adoption into the overall Master Builder's Plan.

I hope you enjoy this book and I hope that it inspires you to take action to help the government of the United States to stand firm against any attacks on democracy from without or from within. Stopping politicians from giving away the resources of the country to buy votes is a good way to start. When President Trump drains the swamp, we intrinsically know things will be better. A little accountability can go a long way.

I wish you all the best

Brian P. Kelly, Publisher
P.O Box 621 Wilkes-Barre, Pennsylvania 18703

About the Author

Brian W. Kelly is a retired Assistant Professor in the Business Information Technology (BIT) program at Marywood University, where he also served as the IBM i and midrange systems technical advisor to the IT faculty. Kelly developed and taught many college and professional courses in the IT and business areas. He is also a contributing technical editor to IT Jungle's "The Four Hundred" and "Four Hundred Guru" Newsletters.

A former IBM Senior Systems Engineer, he has an active consultancy in the information technology field, (www.kellyconsulting.com). He is the author of 136 books and numerous articles about IT topics, sports, and life issues. Kelly is a frequent speaker at COMMON, IBM conferences, and other technical conferences and user group meetings across the United States.

In 2006, Brian departed from just tech books and he began to write patriotic / political books. When this book was first introduced, in its original form, it was his seventh patriotic book and it joined his other great informers: Taxation without Representation, Obama's Seven Deadly Sins, Healthcare Accountability, Jobs! Jobs! Jobs!; Americans Need Not Apply!; and Kill the EPA!

This is Brian's 136th book.

Chapter 1 Should Welfare Be Paid Back?

A never-ending question if at a bar!

Can you imagine being at a bar and you are the somebody who shouts out: "Don't you think welfare benefits should be paid back? You might not get positive credit for the discussion but by the end of the session, morning or evening, you would get enough different answers to make you question your original thinking on the subject. It is a hot potato.

Should welfare be paid back? Among other places, to find that people think about it, I went to the http://www.topix.com/forum, and the first comment was the kind of idea that if brought out in public, would definitely generate a lot of talk. Forums are in many ways places where John and Jane Does can talk anonymously as if they had a few schnorkies in front of them when talking, and who cares? Check out this forum post but a guy who wants to be known as *Why Not*. Mr. *Why Not* gets our discussion rolling with some definite opinions:

Just hit myself in the head with an idea.

On another thread I was trying to explain why a loan was different from a gift as it applies to food stamps and welfare.

Then it hit me. Why don't we make people pay back benefits such as food stamps and welfare? Computers are wonderful (at times) because they can remember anything that is entered into them.

Let's keep track of all benefits people receive in the way of food stamps and welfare, including SSI. If they ever receive a tax refund, lottery winnings, etc. let's take the benefit money back first. Say these people eventually make it big, earn twice the poverty level, etc. make them pay it back. Kinda like child support.

What do you think?

I was fishing for ideas before I wrote my third version of this book, which takes another hard look at welfare accountability. My wife calls it research. So, we are all on the same page, Merriam Webster defines accountability below and then they give the perfect example a group that is rarely accountable:

> Accountability is the quality or state of being accountable; especially: an obligation or willingness to accept responsibility or to account for one's actions. Example -- public officials lack accountability.

In my research, I learned that there are a lot of thoughts on paying back welfare by people who would not give up a penny as well as those who would be willing to give away the whole store. Most have good reasons for their feelings on the issue based on their own experiences in life.

For example, here is a direct response to *Why Not* that is completely the opposite in the feelings it generates:

> Some food stamp recipients are old, elderly and sick living on a fixed income. They may have worked hard all their life, and are really not happy they are on assistance but it's get the assistance or be homeless and hungry. How are they going to pay it back? Especially if they die and have no estate?

> Should the food stamp recipients be pushed off the cliff in a wheel chair?

Let's take a shot at an answer for that question. If I ran the US Welfare, Inc. and the numbers showed that the situation for which the old, sick, food-stamp recipients, living on a fixed income had not improved, then the only correspondence sent to the recipient would be once a summary of benefits sent once a year along with a Merry Christmas note. To do this, of course, the US would have to collect such information. The men in the black coats with the big cars would not come collecting to somebody in dire straits.

Mr. Another Voice on the matter (my name for the writer) chimed in with his thoughts:

> Did you know that some people get back money on their income tax that they NEVER PAID IN?!?! This means that you and I pay in money to GIVE to people for absolutely nothing. Let's stop giving people money they never earned or paid in.

Since the comments in this chapter are important but who sent them is not, all other voices will hereby be known as "AOV" for *all-other-voices-on the matter*. Then I will not have to type so much. Topix.com is where all this stuff has originated.

> AOV: I think assistance should be only for someone 65 or older.

> AOV: So, what do we do for all the children that are being had in poverty level families? It's not the children's fault their parents don't make enough for groceries. But taking food-stamps away from the parents means you're gonna have quite a few hungry babies. Should we send them all to your house for supper?

Paying a debt back when you are able is not freeloading. Unless an individual is physically able to work, and there are job opportunities, and the choose not to take them, their benefits even in a payback system as I propose should not be affected at all.

> AOV: Well if the parents can have them, they need to get there arse out and feed them!! If we give people the luxury of sitting on their arse, they will.

> AOV: I'm not saying everyone has to pay it back. Only those that can afford to do so in the future. Kinda like student loans; they NEVER leave you. If you are a child and receive benefits (the computer knows who you are) you shouldn't be penalized and have to pay it back just because your parents got benefits for you. You've heard the expression, "pay it forward", this is the idea. BTW Medicaid can and will go after your estate when you die if you have no surviving spouse or hardship family members.

I guess I am thinking more in terms of the new recipients who are receiving benefits because of this recession. I would think a lot of new recipients would welcome the idea of paying it back. They aren't used to having to ask for assistance. Even those that are long time hard core "system users" would have to pay it back if (by chance) they got a windfall, great job (I said by chance), etc. in the future.

As my husband says occasionally: "It's an idea, not a good one, but an idea." I thought (again) about this right after the cute little whale dork left.

AOV: And if you take the luxury away they still will be planted on their arses. It's not going to do anything but take food away from the children.

Let me say it again. I am not contesting that it would not be easy to help put people back to work again who have been on welfare for the duration. But, that is why we spend billions of dollars on social workers whose job it is to do a fair job of evaluating who is worthy of receiving welfare and when they should be able to get off and if possible, begin repaying.

AOV: Not everyone on assistance is sitting on their butt and it's rude to say so, many are working full time jobs at that, but their incomes are low, and they need help meeting average living expenses. Yes, there are MANY abusing the system but don't forget many are not. If you were making $40,000 a year and got laid off. Had a hard time making ends meet so you took the first job you could at barely over min. wage & had to apply for assistance how would you like it if people just assumed you sat on your butt all day. There are a lot of different reasons and circumstances that put people in the position to apply for assistance so remember that when passing judgement.

AOV: You are right. I believe there are a lot of people who truly need assistance and are still working. Times are tough now. I also believe a lot of the people applying for assistance now would really be happy to pay the money back when they get back on their feet and have the resources to pay it back. I believe most of the new applicants have never been on assistance before and are working as hard as they can to get off of assistance. My opinion.

As nice as it is to feel compassion for the feelings of those collecting welfare payments from the rest of us, it is not their feelings that matter here. As long as their needs are being met, they should thank everybody and not be concerned about rude people who may not be in such good straits either. When your family is being fed by other families, I think you have to learn to take it on the chin. If you refuse to take it on the job, there is the idea of going out and getting a job. Otherwise, just thank the hand that feeds you. It's the smart thing to do and the right thing to do for being able to live on the dole.

> AOV: People bitch about government handouts, but they fail to mention the 3 or 4 grand they get every year on the earned income tax credit... That's more of a handout than welfare. The max cash assistance you can receive is 240 a month.

> AOV: It's called Earned Income Tax Credit. You get it if you have children and are working. This is in addition to being able to deduct child care, etc.

> I think it is welfare for the low / middle class who have children. They don't call it that, but for those of us who do not qualify (higher income or no children) that IS a welfare check and it comes out of OUR payment into taxes.

> So people, if you get a refund check from "income taxes" that is more than you paid in, guess what: YOU ARE ON WELFARE. So, before you start throwing bricks at the "system users" look in the mirror.

If I were the Boss of Welfare. Inc., I would do away with the income tax credit. This amount does not enter into the calculation that determines the level of welfare one receives and is just a sneaky way Congress has found to pump out another $50 billion of off-the books dollars to buy votes. All welfare should come from the Welfare system, not the income tax system.

> AOV: You folks need to be more like Jesus and help the poor. You people are so un-Christian like. I'mma pray for yaw'll.

AOV: I know a gal who has 4 kids and works about a third of a year because she gets such a large income tax return she doesn't HAVE to work FT all year round....esp with all her housing and lonestar card + medicaid. There comes a point where people like her need to be forced OFF welfare!

AOV note to *Why Not*: You lose. I have NEVER received a "tax refund" more than the amount I paid in. Never qualified because I either didn't have qualifying children at the time or because my income is too high. Although, if I had qualified I would have taken it and never even given it one thought that it was "welfare".

Why Not: Quit pushing me on this. I am your strongest ally on this issue. You pointed this info out in a post several weeks ago. I have taken it from there and have slammed it in the face of welfare haters on at least 7 or 8 threads. I tell them to look in the mirror. They generally quietly leave the thread or derail the post, so it is not discussed.

AOV: Unfortunately, giving parents food stamps does not ensure their children will be fed. Food stamps can be sold for cash, which is then used for purchasing liquor, cigarettes, and drugs.

In many school districts, the poor children are fed breakfast and lunch. In Washington DC, they also get taken care of until 6:30 p.m. and fed dinner. In my community, volunteers fix food packages for the poor children to take home over weekends, so they won't be hungry.

What is being done with all the food stamps these families are already receiving? It doesn't appear they are feeding their children.

IMHO, this is another one of the big rip-offs of the welfare system. It helps parents buy drugs for the child's food rations. There should be no lunches at schools for students to make up for parents who choose not to give their children a lunch to eat. School is for school, not to be an adjunct to the welfare system. Again, this is just another way to put more money into the hands of those who are limited by the welfare caps.

If Parents do not send their children to school with a lunch, the parents probably are abusing their children in other ways and they should be investigated and put in jail. We already pay a lot of welfare workers to make sure our dollars are spent properly. There are remedies, and feeding students at school is not one of the better remedies. If we want the parents to be able to sell their food stamps than why not permit the parents to come in and eat breakfast lunch and dinner at the school and get cash for their food stamps. If that is not what the system calls for then, it makes no sense to give the children meals at school either.

AOV: If I were making $40,000 a year, I would live within my means, which includes putting money away for a rainy day. That is prudent judgement, no matter how much you are earning. If I was living paycheck-to-paycheck, I would not have children until I was sure I could take care of them. I wouldn't expect the taxpayer to pay for my choices.

AOV: Yes, we can thank Barney Frank and Frank Dodd for creating the current housing debacle. Many of the houses that are being repossessed by banks are totally wrecked inside. The people had to put nothing down, so they had nothing to lose.

AOV: I know a young couple that experienced job loss. They tried everything they could with their loan company to get deferred payments, anything to keep from losing their home. They had invested money in it. They did have something to lose. The loan institution told them they would rather foreclose on the house, rather than work with them, because by foreclosing they would receive a $150,000 subsidy from the federal government.

The government created the sub-prime housing crisis by insisting that banks give huge loans to people who could never pay them back. It was a program doomed to failure and intended to pass on a lot of credit to kind Congressmen who do not protect taxpayers' dollars.

AOV: The current protestors against Wall Street are protesting having to pay back their student loans. They are not asking for deferment, or lower payments, they want it forgotten. Student defaults on loans are at an all-time high. The fact that included in the health care, was the complete takeover of student loans by the government versus the private sector, does not bode well for the future of the program.

The problem is our current administration and dems in general, do not want these problems stopped. They only encourage more of the same with more spending and no cuts. There has not been a US budget passed since nobama took office.

The more people the dems can get dependent on the government, the happier they are. They are buying votes. It is devastating our country.

AOV: Wrote about *Why NOT:* Since you are not a registered user, we can't prove that what you say is untrue. However, you haven't made your assertions to look into the mirror on Paris Topix. I have been on many topix locations regarding this subject, and I assure you, while you have people that will support your claims, there are many that would not, and they don't quietly leave the thread, or derail the post.

...

That is that

Was that not refreshing? I sure hope I picked up comments from both sides. I think so. Can you imagine the millions of comments being made each night by Americans on both sides of this issue, who just don't' know any more! Shutting down their ability to speak about how they feel because another may think differently is not the answer for our great democracy.

Well folks, that is that in this chapter. We just served a role as the fly on the wall for a great discussion. In every neighborhood in America and in every neighborhood bar and even the hoity toity bars, the common folk, not the elite, are engaging in simple discussions about how things seem to be to them.

Watching TV, they get talking heads with an agenda throwing big elite thoughts at them. But, when at home thinking, or in the neighborhoods talking, nobody can stop their pure thoughts and they come out just like the thoughts above—not good, not bad… just thoughts.

The best help for a democracy is a continual clear and fruitful exchange of ideas. When people, including my relatives say, *let's not talk politics*, whether it is at the dinner table or on our comfortable chairs and couches, it is the worst advice one can take. Being popular is not the best medicine when our country is at stake. It gives the bad guys a license to create more trouble than otherwise.

Agree or disagree, we owe it to our posterity and history and for the lost blood of the founders, to do our part in this United States to remain vigilant about the rampant chicanery of our greedy political officials. We must talk to our neighbors openly whether they like Trump or Clinton, or not. We need to find some common ground to defeat those who have gotten too powerful for their own good. We the people run this country, whether we know it or not. The warning of course is that one day if we do not discuss ideas, we may have our country taken from us by people with friendly faces and nasty hearts.

Have a few cold ones or some Hot Toddies in the winter and let it all out. Keeping it inside means that the corrupt leaders always win, and God knows they have not been doing anything well for Americans— in the past eight years at least. Don't let them lead our discussions. We know who they are, and we know who their allies in the corrupt press are. We have minds and we can think for ourselves. God bless America!

Chapter 2 Welfare Debate Among Americans

Do Americans care: You bet we do!

There are two sides to every issue. In a debate about welfare conducted online recently the participants were asked whether welfare in the US should be ended. That may be an easy question to ask but it is a tough question to answer.

Many of the debate participants highlighted the abuses of which they know first-hand and also through the tales of others. Knowing that the abuses actually are paid by them through their taxes is naturally upsetting to normal Joes and Josephine's.

Nonetheless, there are those who look only at the good intentions of welfare, and they choose not to see the abuses in the implementation or the greed of the abusers. Such good people do exist though if the world were run according to their precepts, I fear everybody would be motivated to choose to be helpless.

Consequently, there are many opposed to suggesting welfare be shut down completely. This first comment starts out asking us all to check our souls before we answer the question:

"What would Jesus say/do?"

The comments in this debate are put forth with quotation marks and they are indented. My opinions and observations of their comments are shown directly after without quotes and without indentations. I hope this engenders some good thinking among the readers.

"I know it's a cliché to say what would Jesus do. That being said, what would He do? Most Americans call themselves religious and the majority of those would put the check mark on the Christian box. So, with that, why would the same people simple call welfare *lazy people who drain us and basically are a waste of air?* I don't get it. Jesus always spoke about how the weak will be saved and all that stuff. Most Americans would say that they are Christians, but I guess it's easier to say we are something than actually be something."

"Bad things happen to good people, and if the people standing do not help the people that fall down then we are doomed. It's as simple as that. I wonder how many of the people who voted yes have actually been successful in life with absolutely no help from anyone whatsoever. The truth is EVERYONE in life has been helped by someone else, and unfortunately some people have to go to government."

My favorite retort to those who wish we simply increase welfare amounts and forget about what it does to those just getting by who pay the taxes, is coming. It also applies to those who have been able to position themselves as welfare recipients. This comment gives away my feelings on how we should conduct our welfare business in the US.

"I am 100% behind helping helpless people but I am not as much as 1% in favor of making people helpless." Remember the title of this book is not *No Lunch!* The Title of this book is *No Free Lunch!* Why would anybody that has been fed during hard times object to paying something back to benefactors when times for them are better? Answer me that, Riddler?

The following opinion piece strengthens my argument even further:

The poor are better off without welfare. Ask Kansas Gov. Sam Brownback. Opinion piece by Christian Schneider, Opinion columnist Published 7:53 a.m. ET Aug. 11, 2017 | Updated 9:56 a.m. ET Aug. 11, 2017...
https://www.usatoday.com/story/opinion/2017/08/11/cutting-welfare-helps-people-christian-schneider-column/557082001/

Sam Brownback: It is not the good intentions of government programs that matter, it is the bad incentives.

(Photo: Charlie Riedel, AP)

"In J.D. Vance's hit 2016 autobiography <u>Hillbilly Elegy</u>, he tells the vivid story of rural Midwestern whites trapped in a cycle of poverty and unemployment. Preeminent among the colorful characters who populated Vance's life as a young man was his grandmother, "Meemaw," a strong, salty old woman who did not possess a filter between her thoughts and words."

"Meemaw believed much of the poverty in her Middletown, Ohio neighborhood was caused by government handouts that incentivized the poor to not work. Among the invectives she lobbed at her neighbors: 'She's a lazy whore, but she wouldn't be if she was forced to get a job'; 'I hate those f_____ (the government) for giving these people the money to move into our neighborhood; I can't understand why people who've worked all their lives scrape by while these deadbeats buy liquor and cell phone coverage with our tax money.' "

"While intemperate in her observations, new data show that, at least relating to her larger point, Meemaw might have been on to something."

"A study by the conservative-leaning Foundation for Government Accountability tracked more than 6,000 Kansas families 17,000 individuals who were moved off of cash assistance in 2011 when Governor Sam Brownback instituted new work requirements for welfare recipients".

"The data show that families who left government assistance under the new work requirements saw their incomes double within one year of leaving welfare. Within four years, their incomes nearly tripled, as they earned nearly $48 million more in wages than when they received a government check."

Of course, without programs such as those instituted by Governor Brownback, the couch would have remained the home for the eternal couch potatoes in Kansas for perhaps all of eternity. Taxpayers would be paying for their largesse without much impact on the real problem. Moreover, nobody would have known that they could do much better including the potatoes themselves.

In the Welfare debate survey that I cited earlier, there was no opportunity in the survey for an *in-between* answer. **Should welfare in the US be ended?** -- is a pretty straight question. And in the debate, the answers were typically pretty straight forward. They seemed to be based on the responders' pre-dispositions.

I do believe that if the question were: "Should welfare <u>as we know it</u> be ended in the US?", the answers would have been less definite and would have added some of the conditions that would need to change for welfare to be a better deal for both the needy and for the forced benefactors.

The irony in all of this is that the forced benefactors who, religiously pay their taxes every year to support welfare, are also needy. They just do not have their hands out.

For example, some continue to say the biggest attempt on cleaning up welfare as we know it was brought forth in the welfare bill by the Clinton Administration. Some of us are old enough to recall that on August 22, President Clinton signed into law "The Personal Responsibility and Work Opportunity Reconciliation Act of 1996 (P.L. 104-193)."

It was a comprehensive bipartisan welfare reform plan that would dramatically change the nation's welfare system into one that required work in exchange for time-limited assistance. This was a step in the right direction. But, nobody even today has suggested setting up welfare so that it can be paid back when the needy are no longer needy. Why not?

The answer to *why not?* is the focus of this book. It is a major flaw in our welfare system and it feeds the notion that the people collecting are magically entitled to welfare and have no obligation to the people who in many cases have saved their lives.

Just as the group of Americans that I surveyed briefly in Chapter 1, this new group involved in the debate that we are now highlighting, verified my conclusions as I researched this topic. It shows that Americans in general have a mixed reaction to using taxpayer money to finance the well-being of people who do not work or who cannot work.

The perception by many, especially older people, is that those on the dole are lazy or have figured out clever ways to rip-off the system and in so doing, they are ripping-off the older people and many other taxpayers.

I know that there was nothing worse for my father, while I was a kid, than the thought of going on public assistance. Working at Stegmaier Brewery, there were many years in the cold months, my father would get laid off, but he would never go on "relief." He'd borrow money first. He had no problem showing up for the big five-pound boxes of "welfare cheese" or butter or pasta.

Back then, cash payments were called "Relief." As a descendent of Irish immigrants who had struggled to make it in America, while working for slave wages, my dad knew that Americans had to work, or we did not eat. Things have changed. And not for the good.

Sometimes perception becomes reality as what people perceive, they soon learn to believe. I am convinced that nobody has the 100% correct perception of how necessary welfare payments are for those on welfare today but the fact that such recipients are not banging at the treasury door when they get off welfare, to contribute a few pence to help the next guy in need of a handout, tells me something is wrong with our current system.

When you work hard, and you see able bodied people coming through the register line with steak while you are having a hard time not downgrading to cat tuna, perceptions are difficult to control about why that is?

As noted, I found a number of forums and comment areas on the Internet that highlighted what some very normal Americans in regular occupations observed about the 20% of Americans who today are on the doll.

Most people who work, if they do not find a wheel chair or a walker helping the person at the register, are inclined to think that their taxpayer contributions to their welfare support payments is a perpetration. They mince no words in describing it as a plain old rip-off of the suckers who work in America. To many, that sure is what it looks like.

WC Fields often said, "Never give a sucker an even break, and never smarten up a chump." Americans today feel like suckers and chumps as the community organizers and others supporting Welfare, Inc, have an army of lawyers at the ready to bilk normal Americans out of their hard-earned income at the drop of a hat.

Think about that and ask if it is asking too much for the government to keep track of the bills it pays to whom. Let's look at a few stories about that in the next chapter.

Chapter 3 Americans Do Not Always Agree

Grocery cashiers know more than most would believe.

Nobody sees how welfare recipient's rip-off the system more than the cashier at the local grocery store. Some cashiers are very ungracious after work as they report their experiences at the local gin mill. Here is one such story:

> "As if it wasn't bad enough knowing that The Government was giving my hard-earned money to young, totally capable, but unwilling, and lazy, high school drop-outs, I as a cashier get to personally hand out the food that those food stamps and WIC checks paid for to the young and lazy "Useless Trash of America" (as i refer to them)"

> "And I have to do so, to support myself but as a (let's call it a side-effect) I am simply Making more money to be taxed and given to the Trash. It is a horrible cycle, that I am simply SICK TO DEATH of."

> "And as if this didn't grind my gears enough, I work at a very High-end (High-priced) grocery establishment, therefore not only are they buying food with my money they are buying expensive over-priced food. And not essential food like milk eggs and bread, Pop tarts and $5 bags of high-end chips, and Sushi (Pricey anywhere) and

then pull out their own cash (I'm sure they didn't really earn or at least wasn't taxed). In order to pay for their cases and kegs of alcohol and bulk packs of tobacco."

"Now I make no joke when I say I could quite literally go on typing ALL NIGHT, but I will end it here by saying there has existed a single principle since the very beginning of the human species or life itself for that matter that I STRONGLY believe we should follow today. And that saying is, as we put it in the South where I live: "YA DONT WORK, YA DONT EAT!"

Former Vice President Joe and his spouse Dr. Jill Biden are not part of the crowd looking for welfare. But, they have a definite opinion about how much you and I should give to help those not doing so well. They are both well respected big shots in American politics—you know them.

The couple came to my attention probably about ten years ago as tightwads on the charity circuit with about three hundred or four hundred dollars donated together to charity each year. They want American taxpayers to pay the cost of welfare needy and welfare cheats in larger numbers but find no such obligation to chip-in for themselves.

I have heard they are Catholics as am I. The number on their tax form was so small in terms of their charitable donations that they would not have even been able to get credit for being paying members of any Catholic Parish of which I am aware.

Americans can all go to church for free; but you can't escape those dues envelopes and the expected support for your own parish. The Bidens' tax returns spells t-i-g-h-t-w-a-d. Check them out when you have time.

Seemingly because they try to direct billions from the pockets of others to welfare recipients, Joe and Jill Biden have no problem asking you and I to give up healthcare at work to sign up for lousy Obamacare. They also have no problem asking us to accept illegal aliens taking American jobs, such as yours and mine because that would mean you could be a better American by helping foreigners.

Yet, in their scenario, Joe and Jill would give up nothing to help you if you ran into trouble after giving up all your work-earned rights to one of their favored—legal or illegal. Ok, I will take the dogs off the former VP for now but please remember the missive.

Do you believe that? Believe it!

Another fellow in the debate, was disgusted that takers never give anything back. He offered that:

> "People are getting lazier day by day. People I attend school with are on welfare because their parents are too lazy to get a low-end job and work their way up from there. I can't stand seeing my check every month get cut short because people who are too lazy or faking disabilities are getting part of my money that I worked so hard to earn."

> "Now, if people actually were mental then put them on medication so they can work instead of giving them free money. We are in too much debt as it is, growing up thinking I'll be okay, but I forget about my future kids. I'm sorry but some fat chick that has designer jeans, fancy fake nails and an expensive up do doesn't deserve

free money because to me that's cheating all of us hard workers out of our money. My mother works for CVS and sometimes when I go to bring her lunch I see people driving Mercedes and fancy cars, driving up to collect welfare and I sit in my car thinking what in the world? It isn't a free check—It's meant for people that need it. People need to stop abusing it."

Do you see anything like that where you live? I do.

Most people who take the time to complain on a debate, have a long-time perspective about what is going on. They mostly love America and are taken back at how slothful we have become as a nation.

They have friends who think it is better to take from the country than give as JFK suggested. *"Ask not what your country can do for you; but ask rather what can you do for your country?"* Few seem to care unless it makes them feel good and it will be good for them even if it costs somebody else more than they can afford.

Here is another telling comment. This one is similar as it is from somebody ready to give up himself because he feels that too many people no longer care about what is right for America. Here it is:

"This country makes it that so people don't even try anymore! We can't continue like this or we are going to completely cripple our country! If you don't give away free money, then people have to find a way to survive! We have to stop enabling!!! We are going broke too in the social security because everybody thinks they are disabled and stand in line for their money too!!! Have you ever seen some of the people who claim to be disabled?

PEOPLE, go get a friggin job and stop using the system. Whatever happened to the days where family members helped other family members until they got on their feet???? We have lost all sense of family!!!

There are many who are not happy with welfare being so easy to get but they would never consider calling an end to it. They are fearful that in many cases it is needed but there are some politically correct reasons.

I can recall the gangsters in the Untouchables TV series years ago shaking down grocers and bar-owners and whoever. Many of the owners payed them off to avoid trouble. They called it protection money. The irony of course was that they paid the potential perpetrators for protecting them even though they knew the very people who would hurt them if they did not pay were the scum collecting the tribute.

This next comment reminds me of that as this person is suggesting we keep paying off what they believe to be the *n'er do wells*, so that they won't revolt and become wild in the streets, and hurt the rest of us.

They are ready to use welfare as extortion payments. They see Welfare, Inc. joining gangs and extorting the rest of America to get what they now get from welfare. It is food for thought, for sure… but should we pay them off? No way!

"The end of welfare would be the end of civilization in most popular cities in America because the crime rate would sky rocket. The increased crime would end up costing more because more police, prosecutors and jails would be necessary. Housing, feeding and maintaining a prisoner is much more expensive than just giving a fraction of that expense away now as welfare."

Sounds like this person for sure is living in fear simply because bad guys exist in our country.

Another disagreed but you can feel the frustration in his words:

"I feel that if we continue this madness the people are never going to learn and are going to continue on people like me who are making over 100k a year I worked hard in college and at my job why do I have to pay for a drop out who wants to stay home and get stoned?"

Some Americans have something in their craws about some aspect of welfare that gnaws at them. They can't stand it and they take the opportunity to speak out:

"Allow one out of wedlock child on welfare. If pregnant with second, give her the choice of either tubal ligation at the birth of the second, or no welfare on that child. Government could easily afford to pay for procedure and come out way ahead in the long run. Does not affect civil rights--It is her choice."

Being pro-life, I am no advocate of messing with birth rights, but I see the frustration that people see in something they perceive to be wrong. This is a reflection of the thinking that asks: Why does John Doe have a responsibility to pay the sustenance of Mary Doe, who takes no responsibility and makes bad choices even after being advised otherwise.

Why should there not be public dormitories and public soup kitchens that the public supports so nobody starves and so that nobody has a great time on the earnings of somebody else who cannot afford such a great time.

There are those with a great appreciation of history who are upset that their hard-earned dollars go to support those who would never even consider saying hello to them or thanking them for their goodness. Here is one such comment:

"Welfare didn't exist in the US until the 20th century, before that, people who were poor had to work hard to provide for their families, take on another job, and save their money for basic necessities. People on welfare shouldn't be able to comment on this website because they shouldn't have laptops. LAPTOPS ARE NOT NECESSARY. If you're too lazy to work, then beg on the street. The government and hard-working people's wallets are Not Your Baby's Daddy."

If you are reading this book, and I know you are, I know that you know that I think that welfare should not be stopped if there is the slightest notion that a person needs real help to survive. The safety net is very important, so Americans are not dying in the streets.

Yet, many Americans and many illegal aliens have the kindest of us pegged as suckers and chumps and they play us by playing our heartstrings. Having been through some tough times, and never having been on welfare myself, I have a hard time understanding why it would be a reprehensible act to suggest that when one so helped by kind Americans is past their major life hurdle, they should not mind being presented with a bill. Why should they not want to chip in to help others who are in a bad way.

I go further and suggest that we as a nation must begin to keep track of all we give to each person when they are down on their luck. When times are better for the once wretched among us, it is right and proper to ask for a pay back, knowing that more than likely the bulk of it is uncollectible. What do you think?

Here is a very genuine response by what appears to be a thoughtful person:

> "Welfare should not be free money. Why can't it be a job based government organization? "You need welfare, here's a shovel!" Take the drug users and abusers out of the system and use that money gained to fund such a program.

> If your family needs legitimate help then I feel it is deserved, but by no means free. I work for mine, you work for yours! Sometimes I wish I was not so prideful and hard-working that I could sit on the couch to get paid too. Well, we can't all do that... who would pay for who?

Sometimes even those needing medical attention won't lift a finger to help their own families. Here are some thoughts by some good people who have had enough:

> "Working at a Medicaid clinic allowed me to see the able-bodied patriarch of families with five kids refusing to work. Promoting abuse of free healthcare and food benefits without proper government oversight is

disastrous. Create government commissaries that only sell (or ship) nutritious, economical food. Pay for childcare and education, not waste and abuse."

Can there be reasons why Congress would not just say yes to such a proposal. Let the current great grocers in on the commissary action but do not permit the general public to get groceries there. Additionally, the people on welfare should not be mixed in with those who pay for their food with their own money.

There should be a slight stigma for those feeding families on the public dole so that some-day they would be incented to do what they need to do to be a productive citizen. The stigma is a really good thing. Nobody should get too comfortable taking other people's money. And, of course, they should be thankful.

Should having lots of babies be a reason to get a ton more welfare benefits? I surely do not think so. There appears to be no way to shut off the flow of more and more babies because the welfare system grants more dollars for moms with lots of babies than anybody else. Is there a guess out there about why there are multiple generations of welfare recipients with lots of kids? Government is the answer.

Check out these comments:

"My roommate is divorced and the mother has custody of his 2 kids. She re-married and had 2 more kids with another man, and divorced him after 4 months of marriage. Now this single mother gets 2x child support, $1000 in food stamps, about $600 in the form of a welfare check, and free medical. Now she is trying to get more money from the system. Never worked once in her life and is a bottom feeder."

Not looking to punish anybody but like most normal human beings, I have no problem in suggesting that whole families on the dole for generations can eat pretty well in public cafeterias or local food kitchens for meals. Why should it not be hard?

Yes, I do think cities can do better with better bus transportation to take families to the clinics. Yet, I cannot see any welfare program paying for a new car. I can also see movie theatres for the poor in which the movies from several years ago are featured.

The problem is that the government aka Congress wants Americans to be indebted to them for any improvement in their lives. Instead, Americans should fire these representatives to even the score. Nobody in America should go cold nor should they be hungry. However, when things are good, those saved by the system in my opinion should insist on paying back those who are now hurting.

Amen!

Chapter 4 Freedom From Government?

Get your permission slip quickly

Does it seem that more and more of the people you know are looking to become more dependent on the government? Are the freebies so important? Do they want the government to seize most of what they have or were once able to do without a permission slip, when they were free of encumbrances?

Sorry about that! It is now 2017 and the second term of former president Obama is over. I am still spooked by the first term. I almost forgot. We are still mostly free, but many of our freedoms have been under attack and have been compromised for over eight years. Now the DEEP STATE has taken over. Our Constitution needs some re-bolstering. W

Do you want any jurisdiction over your own life? Are you willing to give up control simply because somebody promises a nice dinner and a few drinks? Is your healthcare a right that the government is obliged to provide? Or is it something that you have earned by working for it most of your life? For almost all of the past eight years, a phenomenon that I will call Welfare and Healthcare redistribution has been going on.

Many hard-working people have found that somebody now has an Obamacare subsidy and their own healthcare has become unaffordable or inert with too many deductibles. It is called healthcare redistribution. We have all become victims of government chicanery. We do not notice welfare re-distribution as it comes right out of the tax system; but it is there for sure.

In essence what has happened if that the statists have taken our hard-earned healthcare and they have redistributed it to a more deserving fellow? The statists make the rules. Not many Americans are pleased about giving up healthcare policies for redistribution so that government could offer an alternative that is not what you worked for. Through our representatives, government did exactly that.

Being dependent on government is a big disease today as Uncle Sam and Uncle Barack over the last eight years have teamed up to offer a true opium for the masses. It once was religion, but since many have shut God out of their lives, it now is material goods. To some, government has become the big boss in control of too many things. If government ever becomes fully responsible for any of us living or dying, we will need to plan on having a short-life.

For years after the former president was elected in 2008, there were those members of the low information crowd who believed sincerely that the President was going to give them a pile of cash out of his huge "stash:" Maybe he would even give them a nice new home. It seems like the past president was seen by many who do not engage their minds too often as an all-powerful being.

I watched in 2010 that he became so powerful that he was able to almost single-handedly destroy the best healthcare system in the world. His message was that he would accommodate a mythical few who were, as he said, not covered?

During the past eight years, of Obama times, many Americans began to depend on government. We were constantly reminded of taking care of those temporarily down on their luck? If they needed a house, would you give them yours?

The statists will tell you that we had to nationalize healthcare and create Obamacare to solve the mythical problem of the mythical man who has no healthcare. But, the reality was there was no such man in anybody's neighborhood. It was a myth. Today, your healthcare coverage is diminished and others who did not ever work to have achieved the care you earned, have better care than you. How did that happen?

In helping your fellow man, should you go broke and be OK losing your healthcare. No, of course not but that seems to be what happened. Nationalizing healthcare means that you no longer have yours and I no longer have mine. Everybody has the same.

Well, not exactly. Those very happy with Obamacare have subsidies that you do not get. When socialism takes a country, it means nobody really has anything, including healthcare. Eventually the ants stop working and the grasshoppers have nobody to sponge from.

It is true that there was not much in place for those who needed temporary health insurance coverage. But, a government takeover was not what was required.

Were Obama, Schumer, and Pelosi correct? Did you have to give up your own healthcare so you would really know what the government would provide? Was giving up your healthcare the only solution to help somebody else get some? That's why it is known as healthcare redistribution.

Donald Trump is a breath of fresh air as he thinks you and I should be able to keep our own healthcare. He keeps trying to make it right; yet Congress won't let him. We need to rid the Congress of everybody that makes the life of hard working Americans more difficult. Don't you agree? We need to repeal and Obamacare and go back to the market based solutions of 2010. Then, we can make it all better without redistribution.

After eight long years, many Americans today do not believe healthcare was ever good. Well, everything is relative and having government in charge of our health, as we now have, is not a good idea no matter what our Congress tells us.

If Obamacare was not such a pig, they might have had it running before President Trump took office, but they were incompetent and could not make it work. Hopefully we will have this solved shortly by repealing and going back to the same system we had before Obamacare. It was a system in which hard work and not circumstances and a healthcare lottery decided if you would be treated under government care.

Just so we all know, President Trump believes in the welfare and healthcare safety net for those who need it, not for those who do not need help but want freebies. He also believes in accountability. He is a good man. He believes that we should help helpless people, but he also believes that government programs should not make people helpless.

We all want accountability

Let me say that again. Without government, without any insurance in the world, life can again be as accountable as in olden times. I am not suggesting we cut the cord on everything for sure. The fact is, that when I was a kid, doctors made house calls. When I was not sick enough for a house call, and I went to the doctor as a kid, I had to have the doctor's fee in my pocket when I was seen. The secretary /nurse collected it when I went into the first room. My dad had very little to spend on doctors, but getting well was a priority over everything else.

If somebody needed help before all of the helping hands of government were dispatched, the neighbors, church groups, and relatives would chip in and help—not a government that then all of a sudden believed that it owned you.

When you recovered from illness or a major financial setback, your pride would make sure that you would work off anything the neighbors loaned you and you would pay it all back. You might even throw in a little extra if your full bounty were intact.

The reason so many people are taking from their neighbors through the government today is that nobody asks for a dime back; and we never see your neighbors' faces. Yet, it is our neighbors not the government who helps us through the tax system—even today.

A simple accountability plan would change it so that nothing from neighbors or neighbors through government would be given forever. Everything over time must be paid back. The exception of course is charity when no payback necessary. But, success brings a certain amount of charitable duty when all is well for Americans.

Nobody has a right to take from the tax system, which is America's treasury and not ever try to give it back. Regardless of the laws, if you take "free" healthcare and "free" money and "free" food from the government, inside, you know you owe that back to those who contributed. Government does not create money. They take from Joe and give to Harry. Joe deserves to be paid back when things are better for Harry.

The ideal would be that any citizen, in any kind of financial difficulty, who needs healthcare, would immediately be covered by an enhanced Medicaid, at the outset of the problem. This would require the cooperation of three separate entities: the state government, which would sign off on the enhancement of state-administered Medicaid, the federal government, which would underwrite the augmentation and a third entity, which will be addressed later in this book.

Ironically, the feds have been put in such poor shape that in during the last eight years, the solution would require borrowing from the Chinese, who would be tapped to fund it.

The good news is, that there is no Obamacare necessary. This means we can ditch it 100%. The entrails of the pre-2010 healthcare system need to be stabilized and brought back for improvement. That would mean that whatever is left of the 83% of Americans who got stiffed by the government, would not ever have to move to Obamacare.

After the repeal, those who had moved, would be able to resume life as normal with adjustments for the time spent off track. Even though Obamacare has been "alive" for over seven years, most of its secret objectives of the universal healthcare notion are not accomplished even if government has declared them accomplished. Things are worse; not better. The right idea is Americans helping Americans.

What is Medicaid?

According to the National Conference of State Legislatures, Medicaid can be defined as follows:

Authorized by Title XIX of the Social Security Act, Medicaid is a means-tested entitlement program [this mean that if you are rich, you get none and if you are half-poor, you get a proportional allotment of help] All help right now is funded by state and federal dollars, that pays for health and long-term care services on behalf of eligible individuals (Poor and half-poor).

The program even pays Medicare premiums and, in some cases, other cost-sharing requirements for low-income Medicare beneficiaries, who are known as dual eligible. Medicaid is a good program for sure, but it must be kept solvent by people paying their share of the load—even if it means paying it back later.

Statistics are hard to come by using typical government sources. Total spending on Medicaid in FY 2005 was $316.5 billion. In 2013, the tab was $433.2 billion. This accounts for about 18 percent of total national spending on personal health care. Medicaid pays for a substantial share of the cost of many categories of services. The program, a major source of payment for providers that serve the "uninsured," is the largest source of public funding for mental health and substance abuse services.

Medicaid is also the largest source of health insurance for children in the United States. In 2005, the program covered one in every four in 2005 (28 million). In 2013, along with CHIP, this went up to one out of every three children. Medicaid funds more than one in three births and is the also the largest source of public funding for family planning.

In 2005, the program covered more than 7 million of Medicare's almost 44 million enrollees (about one of every six). In 2014, there were 53.8 million Medicare enrollees, and about 10 million are funded by Medicaid. It provides long-term care coverage for 60 percent of nursing home residents, 44 percent of people living with HIV/AIDS, and 15 percent of all Medicare beneficiaries. Clearly, Medicaid really lends a big helping hand.

Is everybody covered?

The answer to the title question is, "no." Medicaid does not provide assistance to all low-income people. Instead, Medicaid eligibility is based both on financial criteria and on being a member of a certain covered category, including children, pregnant women, the elderly, people with disabilities and certain parents.

Medicaid is a partnership between the states and the federal government and can be characterized as a federally authorized program (in many ways mandated) that is administered by states. States must operate their Medicaid programs in accordance with an approved state plan.

In my research into how the eligibility requirements play out in practice, from speaking with several doctors, including those working in the General Practice, Pediatric, and ER/ Trauma areas, in different states, this is not the spirit of the law.

It does not stand alone either as the EMTALA Law comes into play in emergency rooms to assure all are treated. In the interest of providing a better understanding of my idea of enhanced Medicaid, let's now explore the glory that is EMTALA.

Chapter 5 Emergency Care via EMTALA

Healthcare is a major component of welfare

I have always been confused about the supposed emergency that Obamacare was supposed to solve. I have always been confused as to why Obamacare was so rushed. To me, there was no emergency that needed to be solved in 2010. Today, with Obamacare having taken its toll on many hard-working Americans, there really is a deep need to get something done after seven years of this disaster. Does the word "repeal" strike a chord?

This book focuses on no free lunch for welfare, meaning welfare should be paid back when the recipient is able again. All forms of healthcare provided free are really welfare programs and they too should be accounted and when the patient is ready, a plan to pay the beneficence back should be created.

If the states and the federal government actually believed that there was a need for full insurance stipends for a percentage of the population who could not afford health insurance, then (please think about this), why were these poor people not always on Medicaid. If Obamacare pays for poor people's insurance via stipends above and beyond Medicaid's limits, why was it even necessary when Medicaid was already in place? To ask a bit more succinctly, why stipends for Obamacare when Medicaid and EMTALA were both in place in 2010?

Only about 10 million people are enrolled in Obamacare in 2017, through its online marketplaces, and most of these receive subsidies. Why not just jack up Medicaid eligibility to solve that problem and forget about the huge Obamacare Bureaucracy? Those receiving subsidies are over the Medicaid limit or they would be on Medicaid. The numbers are a snapshot right before Nov. 1, 2017, when individuals began enrolling for 2018 insurance coverage through the law's marketplaces.

Does it not puzzle you as it puzzles me that if the supposed six to seven million who enjoy the Obamacare subsidies today did not qualify for Medicaid by the low-income rules set up by the states and the Feds, then how is it that they now qualify for Obamacare subsidies? Help me with that. Could this all not have been solved by putting the Medicaid limits at the level of Obamacare subsidy limits? Why not? Who needed Obamacare other than the federal government and its sycophants in trying to put Government in charge of our healthcare.

Poor people should be helped by a charitable notion like Medicaid, not a healthcare redistribution scheme such as Obamacare. Right? Was this just another Democrat scheme to pass out government money to the people to get votes? Even Democrats admit that it was.

What about the increased demands of emergency rooms?

Even if you are unaware, if you checked, you would find many illegal foreign nationals in Emergency Rooms. One would think that in tough times, they get a night out of the cold if nothing more. Instead of getting into an emergency room as an emergency, sometimes patients, such as some of my own family members and myself have had to wait as much as 16 hours for service.

Since EMTALA, demands on ERs have mushroomed. Most Americans have noticed the crowds. ERs are now primary care for those here illegally. I suspect that if in the new world of medical help, I experience this myself in the small berg in which I live, then the wait must more than likely be longer in many other more populous places.

For me, this one 16-hour trip was my max time ever, but it is substantially longer in and out all the time any more than the "olden days." Many of those waiting cannot speak English. I do not know under what healthcare plan these folks are entitled? Everybody in America, however is entitled to EMTALA and have been long before Obamacare in 2010.

EMTALA is another reason why Obamacare is not needed. EMTALA was a godsend to all, though it too has been abused and could be made much better.

This great program that for years may have caused the lines in ERs also added to the ability to get needed care in the United States. It is poorly funded, but every hospital seems to make do, even if lines are extended. The program as noted is called EMTALA.

EMTALA stands for the Federal Emergency Medical Treatment and Active Labor Act. It is also known colloquially as the Patient Anti-Dumping Law. This 1986 act was written initially to prevent patient dumping and as such it requires strict adherence to rules designed to prevent patients in ERs or hospitals from being discharged or "dumped" in other locations—such as nursing homes or even other hospitals, purely so that the dumping hospital would avoid the expense of treatment.

Since then EMTALA has become the safety net for many, especially the illegal population and those who have no social worker, who often use the program's benefits as their only means of health care. Nobody wants to die and nobody wants members of their own families to die. EMTALA has been a godsend.

EMTALA, with the full power of the federal government, requires most hospitals (those that accept Medicare patients/payments) to provide an examination and needed stabilizing treatment, without consideration of insurance coverage or ability to pay.

This means that when a patient arrives at an emergency room and asks for attention regarding an emergency medical condition, the hospital is legally obligated to treat the patient. There are consequences most hospitals do not wish to endure if they do not adhere to EMTALA guidelines. As such the program is very good.

Since EMTALA has been the guiding principal since 1986, ER managers, doctors, and other care providers know that EMTALA requires that the hospital provides a medical screening examination along with any necessary stabilizing treatment to every patient who requests it.

Until those obligations are fully met, the patient must remain in the care of the hospital. Under the law, until stabilized, the hospital may not introduce the notion of reimbursement... but many do so, under the covers for survival purposes. Many hospitals have gone out of business because of a major lack of reimbursement.

Hospitals naturally find the bill onerous, but if you read about the patients that hospitals were dumping prior to this bill, your pity for hospitals would quickly wane. You see in EMTALA, the screening examination and stabilizing treatment must be performed without delay.

Let's review the purpose for EMTALA and its history

Emily Friedman wrote a nice article about EMTALA on April 5, 2011, about a year after Obamacare was passed by the Democrats in Congress. The full article can be found at https://www.hhnmag.com/articles/5010-the-law-that-changed-everything-and-it-isn-t-the-cne-you-think. She titled her piece

The Law That Changed Everything—and It Isn't the One You Think

Thirty-one years ago, EMTALA was signed into law, transforming health care in ways that are still being felt today.

While on a visit to Cleveland Ohio on July 7, 2007 in the waning years of his administration, President Bush made this statement: "The immediate goal is to make sure there are more people on private insurance plans. I mean, people have access to health care in America. After all, you just go to an emergency room." Actually, for years, that was my opinion of EMTALA, a great law that has helped many Americans and also many foreigners with no other ability to get help for health problems.

Hospitals once refused to help sick and injured patients

In the early days EMTALA became the solution as the "wallet biopsy." Or "dumping." Very simply, prior to the implementation of the Emergency Medical Treatment and Active Labor Act of 1986, a patient coming into a hospital emergency department often had no legal right to treatment or even an evaluation, no matter how dire his or her condition. If patients could not prove that they had the resources to pay for care, they could be turned away or sent elsewhere—sometimes in a taxi, sometimes on foot. They often suffered adverse health consequences as a result of delayed care. And they sometimes they died. It was cruel and inhumane, but hospitals did this, they say, to survive.

Of course, all hospitals did not engage in this practice? But, too many found it too hard to resist. Because of the mission of so many hospitals, some did not need EMTALA to make them do the right thing in this area. Unfortunately, there were way too many indefensible situations that led to passage of the law.

Friedman writes:

> "Indefensible" is an appropriate term. Ron Anderson, M.D., president and CEO of Parkland Memorial Health and Hospital System in Dallas, was the medical director of the emergency department at Parkland in the early 1980s, and he knew all about dumping. "I would see patients transferred with knives still in their backs, or women giving birth at the door of the hospital, simply because they were uninsured."
>
> As a young reporter in the 1970s and early 1980s, I remember hearing of women in late-stage labor sitting or lying in hospital parking lots, waiting until the baby was ready to be born, when they would then be allowed into the ED. And I heard altogether too many other stories of denial, suffering and death.
>
> Anderson recalls, "I had always said that if I were ever in a position to do something about the situation, I was going to do it." And he did. After he became head of the state board of health, he cajoled, argued and sometimes demanded cooperation from other health care stakeholders to get a law passed in Texas that prevented dumping of un-stabilized patients because they could not pay for care. One of his fellow advocates showed legislators a photo of a woman who had lost her baby while she was being transferred during active labor. "I was a bit of a bull in a china closet. I broke some china back then, but I had to," says Anderson.
>
> He also began keeping detailed records, and found that between October 1983 and September 1984, of 1,897 patients transferred to Parkland from other sites of care, 537 arrived without Parkland having been informed that they were coming. Parkland also recorded calls from transferring hospitals. In one, a physician said he wanted to transfer a

woman with heart failure who was in the ICU. When the Parkland physician asked for more information, the other physician replied, "She does not have any insurance, [and] the hospital does not want to take care of her, OK? This is a private, capitalistic, money-making hospital. They're on my back to have her transferred."

During another call, a physician attempting to transfer a patient told the Parkland physician, "Honey, we're not talking about ethical practice. We're talking about a lady that needs something done that doesn't have the money to do it with… I am dead serious, sweetheart. That's what your damned hospital is there for."

These, and many other shocking incidents, caught the attention of the CBS investigative show 60 Minutes, which, on March 17, 1985, broadcast an episode titled "The Billfold Biopsy," about the dumping of un-stabilized patients at Parkland.

That same year, the Texas legislature finally passed a law requiring all counties to provide for the health care of their indigent residents, and even appropriated some funds to help defray the costs. It was intended to end dumping. Following passage of the Texas statute, more than 20 states passed similar measures, all designed to prevent the transfer of un-stabilized patients because of their inability to pay.

Another important milestone, even though it came after the passage of EMTALA, was the 1986 publication of an article in the New England Journal of Medicine about transfers of un-stabilized patients to Cook County Hospital in Chicago; 24 percent of all transferred patients arrived in unstable condition (Schiff, R.L., and others. "Transfers to a public hospital,"NewEnglJMed, Feb. 27, 1986).

What Does It Mandate?

There are many misconceptions about what the EMTALA law requires of hospitals. It does not outlaw transfers of patients who cannot pay or who are otherwise deemed undesirable. It does not (at least as of this writing) require that hospitals provide all care in perpetuity to a patient who receives an evaluation in the ER. It allows for waivers in some situations, such as natural disasters.

What it does EMTALA require:

- That all patients seeking care in an emergency department be evaluated by a competent clinical professional, and if found having a condition requiring emergency care must be treated until stabilized before any transfer. For women in active labor, the hospital must deliver the baby unless the institution is not equipped to do so (as in the case of a high-risk pregnancy and the lack of a neonatal ICU).
- The hospital to which a stabilized patient (or one who must be transferred because the originating hospital does not have the necessary services or personnel) is to be sent must agree to accept the patient.
- The patient must consent to the transfer, if possible.
- Adequate medical records must accompany the transferred patient

One thing is certain about this law. It does come with a bite. A hospital found to have violated EMTALA is subject to a fine of $50,000 per incident ($25,000 for hospitals with fewer than 100 beds). Offending hospitals also can be terminated from Medicare or Medicaid, although that almost never happens. And unlike some federal health care statutes, EMTALA actually has been enforced. It is not an empty promise.

In my discussions, I have found EMTALA "abuses" by patients being solved by social workers in hospitals cleverly enrolling patients in Medicaid. I do not know how they do it, but many hospitals see it as a way to remain viable as EMTALA costs are substantial with little reimbursement.

What has been the impact of EMTALA?

EMTALA has had both good and bad effects. For the patient, it is mostly all good. It was and is an unfunded mandate, to be sure; but most hospitals were not in the habit of turning away people with emergency conditions before it was passed. Besides, data on what was going on before EMTALA, compared with what has happened since, are virtually nonexistent, and are usually incompatible when they can be found. The factors that led to its birth were anecdotes and policy concerns, not data.

Certainly, emergency department visits have skyrocketed since its passage, from 77 million in 1986 to 127 million in 2009, according to the AHA (the CDC estimates the total of 2009 visits at 117 million; scholars differ). But the population of the United States has grown markedly since 1986, and there was no huge bump in ER visits in 1987 or 1988, after EMTALA went into effect; the increase has been remarkably steady, at 3 to 5 million a year.

Emergency department crowding, especially in cities, certainly has emerged as a patient care and policy issue, but how much of that can be attributed to EMTALA is uncertain. As other avenues to care shrink, disappear or become unaffordable in a tough economy, the ER becomes the only possible option. Although many patients probably could rearrange their lives to seek care in other settings, the ER is still a theoretically convenient, 24/7 site of care—although the fact that many people must wait there for hours raises the question of just how convenient it is.

A recent study found that one in five patients who go to ERs in California leave without being evaluated at all, and there is no telling how sick they may be.

In addition, some hospitals have dealt with EMTALA by avoiding any exposure to it in the first place. There is evidence that some hospitals had no choice but to close ERs, especially again in California. Physician, or investor-owned specialty for-profit hospitals do not generally have ERs at all in the first place.

Friedman wrapped up her story with a chilling finish.

> If the days of the wallet biopsy are over, few would mourn their passing. A most relevant example occurred in Tucson, Ariz., on Jan. 8, when an apparently deranged gunman killed six people and injured 13 others, including U.S. Congresswoman Gabrielle Giffords (D-Ariz.). Among the dead was federal district judge John Roll. In the Feb. 3 issue of The New York Times, Peter Rhee, M.D., chief trauma surgeon at University Medical Center in Tucson, where the victims were taken, said that Giffords received the same care there as any other gunshot victim. "We don't have time or luxury to ask for insurance cards or to know if they are a good guy or how they are going to pay,' he said. "We deal with whoever comes in the door. We don't know if they are immigrants, if they are legal, illegal. We just treat them.'"
>
> It would be nice if hospitals could get properly reimbursed for that. It would be nice if everyone had coverage, so the question didn't even come up. But if EMTALA has accomplished nothing else, it has created a safe haven for those who fall through the cracks, or who have nowhere else to go at that time of day or night, or—gosh!—those patients who have serious emergency medical conditions and need immediate care.

Hospitals have a lot at stake regarding EMTALA, and, so they have built their ERs and they have trained their care providers with reasonably elaborate measures / techniques so as to not violate the prohibitions of EMTALA. On the one hand, hospitals must collect information, or they never will be paid. Despite this financial need, the priority, according to EMTALA, must be on making the patient stable. That sounds about right.

Yet, somebody must pay the bill and most of these bills are not paid according to the federal government. How can that be? EMTALA created a new class of patients called the *Unfunded Mandate* long before the Obamacare mandate.

These patients receive whatever care they need, and it is often very expensive care for which neither the hospital nor the providers will be paid. Of course, the institution and physicians - - must still pay their own expenses, from nurses' salaries to electric bills. The feds insist that they provide service but provide no funds.

Because healthcare is not cheap, very, very large sums of money are involved. For example, at my own medical center, I learned that the cost of uncompensated care for the "unfunded" was $233,000,000, which represented one quarter of the Hospital's entire annual operating budget. There is not an industry in the land where federal law requires them to give away 25% of their goods and services, and continue to stay in business while being prohibited from raising prices?!

That is the plight of hospitals and they have been forced to make do. And, most have developed clever ways to survive that save an awful lot of money while at the same time, doctors, nurses, and hospital administrators are donating huge sums and their time to the effort. This program needs plaudits as well as fine tuning and support from many.

Hospitals are forced to do whatever they must in order to keep their doors open. For example, they differentiate insured patients from uninsured. They use egregious methods such as charging

$5 per aspirin, double billing, creative accounting, up-coding, cherry picking patients, etc.

Many methods are in fact illegal and yet are done every day. Further, hospitals aggressively go after insured patients who have unpaid bills. These are now known as the underinsured.

Value of EMTALA as a safety net

It is not my intention to pull anybody into a philosophical argument on the merits of universal healthcare. I know that I cannot afford the best health insurance for my own family. So, I get what I can and if my net worth is not enough to sustain us in a crisis, then it's time to look for Medicaid. The fact that the EMTALA exists helps us all.

Even though it may not cover colonoscopies and dental care, it is a big comfort to me and many other Americans. I applaud the doctors and hospitals who provide this care to legal Americans and even illegal aliens. Can it be better? Yes, it can, and that's what we should be working on rather than permitting Obamacare to dismantle the entire health insurance industry. Today many hope that all the King's horses and all the King's men with Donald Trump's help can put the health industry back together again.

The EMTALA scenario for a patient

Many people benefit from EMTALA. When a patient arrives, they are either screened or triaged. Hospitals that have adapted to EMTALA know who to move to the "Real ER," and who to move to the ER serving as a clinic. So, successful ERs have adapted to reality to help with overcrowding and ambulance diversions.

In some NYC ER's for example, very early in the patient process, the patient is given a drink and a sandwich. In some cases, this is all they want, as there is an awful lot of abuse in the system, which hospitals have learned to address. Depending on the condition, patients are either admitted or they receive a battery of tests and are deemed okay and they are discharged.

There are also plenty of cases in which people enter the ER simply looking for a couple days' worth of lodging and hot meals. Since the hospitals are used to dealing with these typically "repeat offenders," they have developed a protocol that allows for these "patients" to be easily recognized and discharged, which often results in the "patient" walking to the nearest pay phone, calling 911 emergency and trying again. This is reality and successful hospitals have learned how to adapt and they continue to survive. Yes, it can be better. But it was never bad enough to warrant the destruction of your health care system by Obamacare.

In my recommendation for payback, all aspects of free medical care are collectible at some point. For EMTALA, there is no free care. It just happens that most people walk out without paying. Most repeat patients know the drill and pay no attention to the post-treatment call for information. Because the risk of not being in the spirit of EMTALA are so high, a system in the future would need to use imaging techniques such as retina scans, electronic fingerprinting etc. to collect the patient information for the pay-back database. Where there is a will, there is a way. And regarding a lesson from EMTALA—Necessity is the mother of invention.

Chapter 6 Other Medical Insurances

Enter Medicaid into the process

As noted in Chapter 5, most ERs have social workers available. These social workers know the Medicaid law and one of their objectives is to save the hospital from having to eat any charges. They can, and in fact do, register patients for Medicaid on the spot.

Is it possible that the aggressive sign-ups in ERs results in a rounding up factor for the patient? In other words, in states where the patient would have to be disabled, though not necessarily legally disabled, as in SSI, would a case worker plug in a disability code on the Medicaid application to help the patient?   It is not for me to say but they very well may do so to help their hospital not get stuck with the fees.

A doctor I spoke with from a very large city hospital noted that just about everybody who comes to their ER is on Medicaid, and very few are just EMTALA. It helps the hospital get some compensation for treating the EMTALA patients. Though nobody knows for sure, this doctor's perspective is that many illegal aliens are also on Medicaid.

The Medicaid Law is different state by state, but apparently, there are very few people who visit the ER with just EMTALA assistance. Medicaid in Pennsylvania and the CHIP program are examples where the poor (children at least) do get preventive care, tests, and even dental. It is not really a bad deal. Instead of a family doctor, the patient goes to a special clinic in which they receive excellent care, both as a preventive measure and when they are not well.

Again, with enhancements to Medicaid and to EMTALA, there would be no need for Obamacare and the bankrupting of the treasury and the elimination of real individual controlled health insurance. Add to that unlimited coverage, unstoppable coverage, no preexisting conditions, shopping across state lines, tort reform (malpractice) and a few other tweaks, and everybody wins. For those of us that trust the government less than insurance companies and who trust all doctors intrinsically more than all bureaucrats, adding on to what we have is the best option, without destroying anything other than Obamacare itself in the process.

Does anybody have insurance?

What kind of insurance do Americans have? Here are some categories:

- ✓ **EMTALA et al** - First on the List
- ✓ **SCHIP** -- Not Bad for Kids
- ✓ **Potential Medicaid**
- ✓ **Self-Insured + Potential Private Coverage**
- ✓ **Potential Employer Coverage**

Now, let's take a look at each of these "types of insurance" in some degree of detail.

EMTALA et al - first on the list

We might also call this self-insured or free care depending on your perspective. It is not the best, but it is completely free to the patient (if they choose not to pay.) At a minimum, everyone in this category is self-insured. We all have enough money to buy insurance, until all our worth is exhausted.

We know that the EMTALA requires hospital emergency rooms to provide emergency care without any regard to the ability to pay. In addition to our net worth, this can be counted as additional insurance. On top of all this, in many cities, there is the availability of additional free care. Estimates of the value of free care are from $1,000 to $1,500 per uninsured person per year.

These clinics include Shepherd's Hope, Lazarus Free Medical Clinic, and St. Thomas Aquinas Medical Clinic in Florida. In California, of course, they are bankrupt, and counties were ordered by the Supreme Court to provide essential medical care to residents who cannot afford to pay for it themselves. One might consider that free and also free of Obamacare.

SCHIP -- not bad for kids

The State Children's Health Insurance Program SCHIP is another tool specifically designed for children, though in some states is used to augment Medicaid funding. It was authorized by the Federal Balanced Budget Act of 1997. Its purpose was to extended health insurance coverage to children in families with incomes slightly higher than the Medicaid income eligibility cutoff. The Children's Health Insurance Program Reauthorization Act was signed into law by President Obama on 2/4/09 and it expanded these benefits even further and increased eligibility. Strangely, not all children have been reached by the bill. Those who are very young (less than one year old) and children nearing the age of 18 are the least likely to be covered.

Potential Medicaid

As noted above, the "theoretical statistics" indicate that just about one of every four "uninsured" persons who is eligible for

Medicaid or SCHIP (for children) for some reason has chosen not to enroll. The unpublished statistics appear to be substantially higher -- perhaps 3 of 4 or better. CHIPS percentages would be even higher because it supports children whose parents earn from 1.5 to as much as three times the federal poverty level in some states.

Medicaid enrollment is a mere formality and in fact can often be done, as noted previously, right in the ER. In many states, it can also be done several months after the care has been delivered. I am not suggesting that there is any chicanery going on here, but the doctors I spoke with said that they were fairly sure that most of their walk-ins were Medicaid.

Self-Insured + potential private coverage

Many people with higher incomes simply choose not to buy insurance for themselves or their children. At their income levels, they are effectively self-insured. Rush Limbaugh for example noted on his program that he carries no insurance.

When an illness shows up at the doorstep, through hook or crook, there is also the possibility of buying private insurance. Some of the real numbers show that about one-third of the uninsured are in households earning $50,000 or more, and more than half of those earn $75,000 and up. These people can clearly afford to buy their own medical care directly and they can certainly afford insurance.

They don't need Obamacare, but Obama has them in the justification as if they have no insurance because they are too poor. That is chicanery for sure. But, when your objective is to take over healthcare and not to make it better, such chicanery is a necessary part of the government package.

Six states have guaranteed issue and community rating in the individual market. In other states, many are protected by the Health Insurance Portability and Accountability Act (HIPAA) and many have access to state subsidized risk pools allowing access to private insurance after illness has occurred. Sorting out how many people potentially have access to different types of private coverage would be another useful Census function.

Potential employer coverage

If Al Gore were writing this, he would suggest that the 800-pound gorilla in the room, which he would call the inconvenient truth, is that about 80% of the uninsured are living in a household with someone in the labor market. At least one fifth and perhaps as much as 25% have been offered coverage at work, but turned it down. They chose no insurance to avoid the cost of their contribution in order to have more disposable income. Quite frankly, so would I if I were 22 years of age. Yet, Obama included these refusers in his healthcare justification.

If the need arises, they can always enroll. Also, since it is easier to get a job when you have one, many who already have a job can probably land one with employer-provided coverage (if needed). Some might even be able to renegotiate with a pay cut to have their employer provide insurance. It helps to know that the HIPAA law prohibits employers from denying employees (actually anybody) coverage because of their (or a family member's) health status.

Despite how dire the need for Obamacare would appear to be in the low-ratings media, the fact is that in general, in America, it is surprisingly easy to get someone else to pay your medical bills - even if you don't have a Blue Cross card or Obamacare.

http://www.ncsl.org/default.aspx?tabid=14052#who

What is my point in all of these statistics? The fact is that Obamacare was justified to the masses as if nobody had health insurance when in fact, based on the discussion above those who do not have health insurance other than the terribly poor have simply refused coverage for one reason or another. They want either you or I or both you and I to pay for their healthcare insurance, and of course Obama in his day, wanted that also.

Who pays for EMTALA?

Now that we know what EMTALA is and we know that the patient is supposed to pay for EMTALA care, we are staged for the next part of our discussion. Before we go there, let us again acknowledge that the EMTALA patient often gives a bogus address and is not required to show identification. Therefore, much of the time, the bill for EMTALA winds up being on the back of the ER or the ER doctor.

Some ER doctors donate as much as $100,000 per year in unreimbursed ER care. Anybody getting care for free in our system should be required to provide valid identification to help assure that there will be an ER there when they choose to benefit from EMTALA the next time.

Here is a story from 9/4/2016.

> Just today I went into a grocery store nearby and I bought a few items. The total was less than $25.00. I paid by credit card. I had a thing called a gold card which I used to get a discount on certain items. Almost everybody at this store has one. I then gave my credit card, which has a chip in it for better authorization. I then signed the signature pad.

> So, there were already three proofs of who I was. The store clerk then asked me for ID. People all around me at various checkouts, who were on welfare, had a thing in their

possession called an Access card. It did not have their picture. They did not have to show ID. Just saying!

They did not need additional ID. I rummaged through my wallet holding up the line looking for my driver's license. I could not take my merchandise home without having that card. So, I needed four forms of ID. Yet, EMTALA patients and voters somehow would be disenfranchised if they were required to have ID? What about not being able to eat. I say everybody has an ID especially the poor because that gets them their food. So, who are we kidding America?

Who pays for Medicaid and SCHIP/CHIP?

States and the federal government share in the cost of Medicaid and CHIP. The federal share of a state's Medicaid expenditures is determined by a formula. The formula itself has a name-- the Federal Medical Assistance Percentages (FMAP). CHIP is different, but includes the notion of sharing. The law recognizes that some states are poorer than others. States with per capita incomes below the national average receive larger federal matching percentages, and those with per capita incomes above the national average receive smaller matching percentages. Every state receives at least a 50 percent match.

States are not required to participate in Medicaid, although a large financial incentive exists to do so. Currently, all states have a Medicaid program except Arizona, which has what is called a "special demonstration project." In essence all states have Medicaid. If a state chooses to participate, Medicaid is an entitlement to the state as well as to individuals, as long as covered services are provided to eligible people in accordance with federal statute and an approved state plan or waiver. In other words, the federal government will pay its share of the Medicaid costs as long as individuals covered, services provided, providers reimbursed, and rates paid are consistent with the state's Medicaid state plan or specific waivers approved by the federal government.

The federal government should give us all a tax break and let the states collect from their own residents to fund Medicaid. It would actually not cost as much when we took out the big bloat from the federal government employees.

The big three do not pay for Medicaid/ EMTALA?

In very few of the magnificent programs designed to help the poor and even those above the poverty level to afford healthcare, are the big three sources of bill paying that I learned growing up. Everybody is very familiar with these three. They are "Me, "Myself," and "I." They do not pay for Medicaid or EMTALA. They do pay for Medicare.

Isn't that hard to believe? If you delve into some of these programs more deeply you would find some requirement for co-pays and small payments, but as a rule, there is no requirement to pay at all. It is a free lunch on the taxpayers for good Americans who are poor, cheating Americans, and illegal aliens. Even when there is an expected payment, as in EMTALA, as my father would say, "Try and get it!"

The fact is that you cannot get blood from a stone. Nobody is suggesting that. But, wouldn't it be nice if the person receiving the service helped in some small way, before, during, or after receiving the care or the insurance/ coverage? (Let us be reminded here that Medicaid and CHIP serve much the same function as insurance.) If the patient actually was expected to participate in the payment of the life-saving services rendered, or the fee for having an insurance safety net, the patient would then be called accountable.

Chapter 7 Accountability

Pay it back, Mac

Right now, the patient is basically not accountable and the
"Kentucky Windage" from the programs quietly implies that the
patient need not be concerned about the mundane notion of
paying somebody else back for their labor, which in turn
permitted the patient to survive.

This is called accountability. The purpose of this book is to
discuss Welfare accountability as it pertains to the recipient of
any federal or state benefit as well as patients in the free health
system. It also pertains to John Q. Public's (that's you and I) and
our ability to keep track of what is owed. Without a tally, clearly
there can be no payback.

The objective for all Americans is for everybody in America to
be accountable so we are not throwing billions of dollars at a
problem and never ever expecting to get anything back for our
dimes. What about Lottery winners and folks down on their luck
in their twenties who make it big in their forties. It will pay off
big in making all citizens accountable. There is no free lunch!

Personal Accountability Record

For this all to work, we would need to implement something
that I have labeled A Personal Accountability Database (PAD)
which would include the Personal Accountability Records for all
citizens of the US, and those who are permitted to use our "free"
services.

The purpose of the PAD/PAR would be to capture the bills and the insurance payments and hold the net balance of anybody who has not paid a qualified health bill, such as EMTALA, a Medicaid or CHIP co pay, or a Medicaid "premium," or any cost, such as Food Stamp purchases, picked up by the taxpayers, typically through government. Healthcare is not free. Food is not free. Insurance is not free. It costs the provider to be able to provide the products and services and it costs the public to pay for those who do not pay.

Your personal accountability ledger in the sky

I had originally thought of the term, Electronic Billing Record as the name for the database in the sky. However, it had already been taken for another purpose. Physician Practice Management Systems (software) have their own subsystems called Electronic Billing and thus, they have Electronic Billing Records. So, now that you know what I am talking about, here is what I propose we call, it the "Personal Accountability Record (PAR) in the Personal Accountability Database (PAD). PAR/PAD then will mean:

- ✓ **Personal** -- Stored on behalf of an individual American
- ✓ **Accountability** -- An accounting of what you owe. -- All patients are accountable for their unpaid welfare charges – medical or normal welfare.
- ✓ **Record** -- A group of facts about an individual
- ✓ **Database** – The totality of the records and files

These records can be used to hold all the amounts owed for an individual "patient" from all health sources covered-- such as EMTALA and Medicaid, Assigned Risk, or whatever is deemed appropriate. Additionally, the records for an individual would also contain all welfare transactions such as Monthly Access Card amounts, cash payments, etc. Additionally, another database can be joined to the Personal Accountability Database to store payback payments made by the welfare recipient. This database can be referred to as the Payback Database.

A good systems engineer, and more than likely a good team of such engineers would be required to design the overall system to be implemented incrementally.

The notion is very feasible and with today's technology it does not have to cost a zillion dollars. It should pay a large part of its cost itself, and eventually, as people get back on their feet and begin to make payments, it can become a revenue generator for the people as a payback. As you may know, this money remains unaccounted today, and thus, all of it is uncollectible, even if one a welfare recipient or a patient was inclined to pay it back.

Do you know of anybody who may have won the lottery, who then immediately writes a check to the government? If the government is not counting, asking, or demanding, logic suggests that the government is not going to get a dime from the winnings, even though the person, once down on his luck, becomes capable of paying something back.

The Personal Accountability Record for an individual would live as long as the individual lives and at least the unpaid charges / welfare benefits for the individual would live just as long. Any collection revenue provided from the PAR system would help provide funding for healthcare. All people would be expected to pay for their own healthcare -- legal and illegal, poor and rich, eventually. Of course, many would not be able to do so and just as today, for these people, the amounts would be uncollectible.

Of course, the record may live longer than the person as there may be living relatives who just might be inclined to pay off the debt of a deceased former welfare recipient or a patient so that their lifetime PAR is clean.

The simplicity of the idea is as simple as "Field of Dreams," the movie. You may recall the ball park notion in the movie, and the catch line that has been used in many ways ever since, "If you build it, they will come." To match the catch line in that popular movie, the American Welfare System and the American Health System can adopt a few catch lines such as the following:

- ✓ "If you keep track of it you will know what they owe."
- ✓ "If you know what they owe, you can bill them."
- ✓ "If you bill them, they will pay."

Pre-Billing

In the early days of computers, there were a lot of schemes that involved unscrupulous experts trying to increase their clandestine revenue. One such scheme, I called pre-billing. When I would instruct new data processing students, I used pre-billing as a ruse topic. I initially defined it as companies billing random customers before they ever received an order and surely before they shipped anything. Students were astonished as it was a prevarication. I did get their attention.

There actually was a real notion of pre-billing which meant that a copy of the order pick-list in a warehouse operation would also be used as the bill to the customer. This was called pre-billing because the bill was ready before the goods were even picked. Yes, I joked with my students that pre-billing meant that charlatans and rogues would send out bills randomly to companies. In other words, they billed before they provided a good or service.

Because the Accounts Payable (A/P) systems in the 1980's often were not fine-tuned, quite often the rogues and the charlatans would get a check from a reasonably high percentage of the companies that that they had illegally billed. Most companies did not check bills thoroughly like they do today. If they received a bill, they simply paid it. Many American households work the same way.

The point is that the A/P departments in companies had to receive a bill to pay it. Some did not have purchasing systems, which would have helped them know what they had ordered. Even if a company receives an illegitimate bill today, there is still some level of propensity for the company to pay it, though this does not happen often-- as much as it once did.

The same propensity exists in US households. When an official bill from the government—especially the government, shows up in the mail box, there is some chance that it would be paid regardless of what it is about.

Now think of all the folks who one day needed EMTALA or Medicaid, who went on to get a college degree and then became a millionaire or at least got comfortable in their lives. They would have full capabilities to pay even an old medical bill or the value of their Medicaid support, if there was a record of it. Today, nobody, even millionaires, pay because nobody keeps track of the bill. I was very surprised that we do not even track those whose bills we pay, whether or not we choose to bill them.

No poll tax

Today in America, everybody over 18 who is a citizen has a right to vote. Let's say we have the PAR/PAD system in place and we have a PAR record on file including every individual's EMTALA bills or unpaid Medicaid charges. Without trying to create an elitist voting class, theoretically, we could explore permitting only those over 18 who are paying their minimum PAR balance regularly to vote.

I am not sure that it is a good idea as stated, but it would be good to have an incentive for all to pay back Medicaid or EMTALA when they can—at least at a minimal level. The fact is there is a risk in a dependent society with fewer and fewer contributing and more and more taking from the system that conceivably at some point it would be the takers, and not the givers, who would be determining how much they get by voting.

Just as a poll tax is not fair, citizens not pulling their fair share should not demand payments through the electoral process from anybody for any reason.

Please note that this is not a well-formed thought and it may have more trouble spots than positives in implementation. So, I put it out, just as a thought, not as something that I would necessarily recommend. I'd love to have input on this. What do you think? Should people who only take from the system be able to vote for their favorite "give me more" politician?

The generous, beneficent, and magnanimous are welcome!

Those who are much better off than most of us may be encouraged by the system managers to contribute to the PAR fund as a charitable donation. This is a far more worthwhile donation than the government's latest call for donations to pay off the National Debt. I'll bet somebody gets their checkbook out and sends in a few bucks. Bill Gates and Warren Buffet combined could not make a dent in the National Debt.

The so-called "rich," with the adoption of the enhanced Medicaid and the PAR, at least theoretically, would not be taxed through the nose by Obamacare. Perhaps even Democrats, such as Joe Biden and Al Gore, could be encouraged to donate to a PAR Trust Fund.

Any donor to a PAR could pick specific people randomly or they could pick people they know, or they could apply their donations on account. At the end of each year, the "on account" donations would be applied to all PAR accounts in the same proportion, or the same amounts, and the PAR system would pay those who had provided the service if they had not otherwise been reimbursed.

The real conundrum, can politicians get credit?

As discussed, the invoice for all "free" healthcare, provided by enhanced EMTALA or enhanced Medicaid, would come due immediately upon the individual recovering and being financially capable. Payments would be reasonably small based on income but there would be small payments even for those on welfare. Eventually a good many invoices from such individuals would be paid using the PAR system, run by a consortium of doctors and patients.

Those who cannot pay their "welfare bill" or their "insurance bill," would be given the welfare or insurance as a loan automatically from the PAR system. Again, it would eventually be paid back by the individual when they got back on their feet.

Remember, there is no free lunch. In the "loan" scenario, there is no politician who gets credit for giving anybody anything other than a loan.

I am conservative, but not exactly like Barry Goldwater, and I am not a Republican, nor am I aspiring to become one. Mr. Goldwater ran against Lyndon Johnson in the 1960's. I am not going to run for President, nor am I going to run for Congress again.

Though I heard it often, Goldwater's message did not reach me and impact me as a teenager who loved JFK and wanted to believe that LBJ would provide more of the same JFK-ness if needed. I remember hearing and seeing that catch phrase in the Goldwater campaign: "In your heart, you know he's right." I knew then that I wanted nothing to do with Goldwater because in my heart, back then, I thought he was full of crap. I do feel differently at this time about Goldwater. In my heart, I am positive Trump is right.

In your heart, you know this is right

I am more knowing now than then, and much more conservative. JFK was the best, as many people today see Obama. Regarding the PAR proposition, I keep thinking that if I say something profound like, "In your heart, you know the PAR, the *no-free-lunch-system* is right," there's going to be a young whip like my former self calling me on it. I would have called out JFK's detractors when I was a teen. But, the fact is, "in your heart, you know I am right." Obamacare must go!

Does this hurt the opportunity of an American individual to receive healthcare? Picture a doctor's office shutting out any patient. I can't. Everybody's life should be saved when they ask for help. There should be no hesitation or delay in health service. Likewise, nobody else should have to pay for that person's trip to the dispensary. Hopefully their life is saved even if they can never afford to pay it back.

Who pays for the free lunch?

In the real world, that which is called a free lunch means that somebody else has given up a lunch or its equivalent. When government coercion is involved, through the innocuous term, "taxation," this is simply not fair. In Robinson Crusoe's world, fiscal goodness meant, "he didn't borrow or lend." Why not keep track of what everybody takes from the system? It does not mean that we will ever collect, but why not try to collect some day? What is right is right!

Too many interested third parties

In a simple plan to keep track of what those who at one time were needy take from society, what is the downside? Those who benefit can pay back the amount taken when they are no longer needy. The problem or downside is that there are many interested third parties involved. I would bet there would be no problem on the patient's' side. Patients just want to get well and stay well.

So, what is the downside? Just one really big thing! It does not serve the purposes of the special interests with huge agendas. They have a lot of political capital invested in Obama-style health insurance. People helping themselves might mean big government is not needed, and then, what would become of our fine politicians?

Moreover, keeping track of what the once needy owe the public does not push forward the need for a single payer health insurance system (government controlled) as passed, in March 2010. In the future: Whatever the agenda-driven Democrats call it right now, the objective, according to Michael Moore, liberal protagonist, is a single payer system. Next time you hear the term, "single payer system," if you love the Democrat Party more than your family's health then say "aye." But, if you love your family and your life, say "no" as quickly as you can.

It may be called a public option, a consumer option, a Pelosi option, a Hillary option, or whatever, and it leads to a single payer system. Based on your own knowledge of government and the needs of the power brokers, do you think that those who want power, not healthcare, want any distractions to their

takeover plan? Now, we have come full circle and we are back
to our discussion of the PAR system.

Do you think they would really go for keeping track of the cost
of enhanced Medicaid or enhanced EMTALA or any of their
"gifts" of your money to other citizens or non-citizens? Do you
think when politicians give the gift of your money to someone
other than you that they want you to get the credit? Where
would the politicians who promised their voters something for
nothing go if all of a sudden, the recipients of the politician's
gifts had to pay the gifts back when they were able? That's why
the "loan idea" will not fly in the Congress of the United States.
For the people's sake, however, it should.

Those who benefit would love to help

Despite the politicians, the reality is that there are few
millionaires among us today who were once on EMTALA or
Medicaid. But there are some. The sin is that we do not even
know who they are. Should we not know this at some level?
They took from the public treasury to make themselves well and
now they are in the position to help twenty or fifty others.
Should they help?

Because no accountability records have ever been kept, we
cannot even ask them for a little help, even if they were inclined
to give it. More than likely, they do not even know the dollar
value of what they received, and I bet as good Americans, they
would be tickled to help if asked.

We can send a man to the moon and did so first—way back in
1969 and still we do not know who we have helped with welfare
or medical services. I think they would pay their bill if we were
to bill them. I would also bet that there are a number of
hundred-thousandaires, and multiple ten-thousandaires, who
may now feel just fine, who we the people helped at one time,
who otherwise may have died. I think they would have no

problem paying their health bill from even ten or twenty years ago if we knew the amount and could be asked for a small payment at a time. But, we do not even know who they are.

Commonsense reforms, not a takeover

Like all spiritual individuals who believe in God, I would advocate promoting common sense reforms that help make health care more affordable for all, to reduce the number of uninsured Americans, and to increase the quality of all health care. Nothing good happens overnight so I would not suggest that anything be done in a hurry, but rather after lots of discussion, lots more town meetings, and lots of prayer.

As I have said more than a small number of times so far in this book, we must first remember that despite the rhetoric on the hard left, nobody in the US is without health care. With just a few tweaks rather than a full dismantling, the care would be far better than the care that Obamacare might yield and it would be fairer, with no gatekeepers. This whole pretend crisis was simply an Obama power grab. Trump will be deep-sixing it soon and I can't wait.

Chapter 8 Personal Accountability System—Phased Implementation

Designing system from top and work down

This section talks about how a professional would design the PAR system so that it would accomplish the objectives for welfare and healthcare. This is just to set the table for what would be necessary to keep track of everything if we can talk our Congress into keeping track of charges made by individuals. The charges would be stored in the Personal Accountability Database.

The state of all healthcare software for practice management, for veterans and other government-run systems, is described well with these two words—hodge-podge. This patchwork of good intentions can continue doing its job, where applicable, while a new system built from the top down is implemented. The first phase of the implementation for medical would be the design and construction of the Electronic Health Record Database (EHR) This would use the best of breed existing systems design plus all of the non-implemented approved enhancement requests. Additionally, room would be made for future notions that would not be online in the short-term.

Design the databases

The second phase would be the design and construction of the PAR databases. This is the Personal Accountability Record, which in a normal business, might be called Accounts Receivable. The PAR database would be simpler than the EHR database to design and build.

In many ways it would take on the shape of a sophisticated open item accounts receivable system in which all unpaid charges from all approved sources would be posted as due. The database would also hold payment information and adjustments that have been applied to any particular bill. Each patient or welfare recipient would have a total balance owed that cross-footed to the total of all the charges, adjustments, and payments. This would assure the accuracy of the system. Each time an account is updated, the cross-foot would occur, and once a day, a cross-foot would be performed on all accounts. The big difference between this special accounts-receivable system and any other is that the payee could be different for every billing entry.

Who would use the PAR system?

We may have patients from assigned risk insurance companies, and the Consortium has agreed to account for these perhaps indigent medical bill payers. The scenario would include the Insurance Company having paid the hospital or the doctor for radiography service, for instance, but the patient has chosen not to make the co-payment or, for some reason, has defaulted in their payment to the insurance company.

If this were an approved scenario, the PAR database would need to be built to store the relationship between the care provider and the insurance company that has paid some or all of the bill to the care provider. For such transactions, the PAR system would need to be designed so that it could assign the bill for payment to the proper party, if it is ever to be collected.

I would expect that insurance companies would be happy to pay the PAR system for collecting unpaid balances and this would be a source of public treasury revenue. Quite frankly, I do not know whether I would want the PAR system to go that far, but it is conceivable, and the software can be designed to be very accommodating.

Any Medicaid transaction would be posted as unpaid and the EMTALA balances, after the hospital or other provider has tried to collect them, would be posted as open and unpaid to the provider. Some methods would need to be developed to determine the split between the state and the federal government but that would be a political thing, long after the technical pieces to accommodate the scenario were in place. Welfare charges to the system would be processed in a similar fashion.

Patient payments would be able to be made via check or credit card or in person to any participating PAR provider for any PAR bill. Just like the banking system reconciles checks from banks all over the world, so also can a PAR type system be built to reconcile the from / to of payments from across the US.

The objective, of course, would be for all providers to be participating. Small fees for collection of debt that was not theirs could be given the onsite institutions (care givers typically). Initially, a servicer should be used to handle the checks and money orders that would be mailed directly to the PAR facility and to provide "customer service."

As the volumes of transactions are better understood, the PAR enterprise of the big system in the sky would need to be staffed with enough clerical personnel to handle the processing of the checks and money orders. Third party customer service in America may be the preferred long-term solution, and, inadvertently, provide plenty of American jobs on American soil!

Again, the intent of the PAR subsystem would not be to be an active collection agency for all providers. Its primary purpose would be to assure that any unpaid medical bill, regardless of its source, EMTALA, Medicaid, or anything else that is authorized, is associated with an individual and listed as due in the PAR database until the person dies.

There could be a small processing fee for Medicaid or for EMTALA or any government mandated act of charity for a patient, collectable only if the patient or holder of Medicaid insurance makes payments. Hospitals and clinics and other providers that are not part of the ownership of the organization, who wish to use the power of this system to collect co-pays, or other fees, if such work were approved, could be assessed a small charge for such services for each item collected.

In addition to the practice management software, this would be another source of revenue for this new public consortium enterprise. Obviously, the database in the sky would need to be designed to handle all of this and more.

Using the right implementation tools

Prior to writing the first version of this book in 2009, my last book was The All-Everything Operating System, (type in the title and you will find sources on the Internet).

As a lifetime computer systems engineer, my recommendation for computer systems would be any platform that could run the All-Everything Operating System, known in the industry as IBM i. This huge system would handle transaction processing and database processing. The requirements transcend the capabilities of Windows systems, and thus it should be created with an easy to use and powerful operating system unlike UNIX, Linux, or any mainframe flavored version. Again, I recommend IBM i.

I would recommend programming in the RPGIV language, the finest business language ever developed. To make coding even simpler, I would recommend contracting with IBM to enhance the language with a natural Web interface to the RPG language running under the All-Everything Operating System, IBM i. The job would be simpler to accomplish with these tools and much less likely to fail.

Question from anonymous reader: Can you tell me a little more about this Personal Account Record. I don't see that in anybody else's Health Technology literature of the day?

More on Personal Accountability Record

The same private HIPAA compliant consortium that handles the Health Records (EHR), would also support PARs. Each time a doctor updates their office system, for example, the software can also be set to send the billing and payment information to "the system in the sky."

The billing and payment information would update the patient's Personal Accountability Record and log the amount due for any type of patient, including Medicaid patients. Emergency rooms under EMTALA would also have access to the PAR subsystem and would be able to update it with any billing data for which the patient is responsible

Once formed, the same doctors who had initially enlisted would "own" the PAR/PAD Company. Insurance companies would be able to interact with the company under rules specified by the board, comprising, as described above.

Individuals would be able to pay any company with a PAR affiliation for any of the balances they may have accrued, regardless of the source of the service. Electronic Funds Transfer System technology (EFTS) would be used to distribute the cash to the proper end-points.

EDI would make it smooth

EDI (Electronic Data Interchange) transactions described in more detail previously, would need to be designed for providing conversational input and output to/ from the PAD/PAR systems. Once the transaction types were designed, just as in regular business EDI systems, conversations between the PAD/ PAR system and the practice management systems used in all provider shops (Doctor's Offices, labs, etc.) could theoretically begin.

Software vendors wishing to participate would have to incorporate the new transaction types within their packages in order to participate. Therefore, the PAD/PAR system would not force any existing software company to go out of business. Everybody would be welcome using new standard EDI formats.

Get a New Tire

Eventually, after patching an old bicycle tire / tube so many times that there are patches on patches and the whole tube gives the appearance of being no more road worthy than a bubble gum tire. Everybody must eventually yield to the purchase of a new tube or a new tire.

Too many little messes out there eventually create one big mess. This big mess is not going to get fixed by fixing one little mess at a time. In fact, it may get worse. So, it really is time to replace it all, but not all at once. Regardless of how good the new systems may be, the big bang theory of software implementation does not work well.

All "at once" projects are doomed to failure. The only thing that the big bang theory ever created that was usable was mother Earth. At the time of the hypothetical big bang, this earth had no people on it; so, the big bang in many ways was a reset to zero with no systems active.

The big bang theory would not work if government took over all health insurance immediately and it won't work if we pull the plug on all other software when we get the PAD/PAR system and the office systems up and running. The ticket to success is incremental implementation.

The design of the end objective databases to hold health records, as well as patient account records, accommodates the highest level of software function that could be achieved by any medical practice management system (MPMS).

The EDI transaction definitions and native support in the PAD/PAR system would permit any and all software to be able to interface with this new high-level facility. In other words, without touching the guts and basic logic of any software system out there, by adding a few EDI transaction types to the mix, the dream of PAD and the benefits of PAR can be achieved. Though none of it may be done licketty-split, it would not be a forever undertaking either.

Moreover, as an added benefit, small practices that choose to use the simple MPMS system would immediately have electronic records at their fingertips. Additionally, the new enterprise could make a small amount of revenue by renting the MPMS software access to the small practitioners at a phenomenally low price and to others as needed at going market prices.

Additional proof that the system is workable

Cash transactions at an ATM, or checks electronically sent among banks, use a similar notion to EDI called the Automated Clearing House (ACH) and a protocol called the Electronic Funds Transfer System or EFTS. Financial institutions not only send information using EFTS, but through the central ACH, they can distribute real cash transactions among many banks or financial institutions who are members of the Automated Clearing House. In many ways, our American banking system is based on EFTS working flawlessly with EDI as the underlying transaction formatting protocol.

You benefit also when you receive a check, such as your paycheck via EFTS. Senior Citizens get their social security checks directly deposited using the ACF and EFTS. EFTS is so similar to EDI that over time the names were merged and it is now known as EFTS/ EDI.

Why is this important? The fact is that the underlying systems to support electronic messages and electronic funds transfer are in place. It may be that an existing EDI format might be able to be used to accommodate the PAR system for input and acknowledgments.

If not, the base EDI transactions can be modified to support the function and be made to take advantage of the existing infrastructure for provider to PAR/ Clearinghouse communication.

Hospitals and clinics probably would have no problem communicating to the PAR clearinghouse, but private doctors may very well have initial issues. That's why we recommend the building of the MPMS system by the Consortium. To handle billing transactions and payment transactions and even adjustment transactions, EDI forms can be modified, or built from scratch, permitting small doctors' offices to participate in one of the most exciting undertakings ever implemented. Let's hope Congress does something like this rather than take over the whole system. Let's make sure we undo the Stimulus language that removes the public from any rights to their own medical records.

End Note

Well, ladies and gentlemen, that is about it for the healthcare accountability portion of this book. I hope you liked it. Throughout this book, we gently coasted to crescendo.

We discussed the reasons why the local and remote medical records systems and the database in the sky have great value in reducing medical errors, especially those that can result in the death of the patient.

The groundbreaking material in this book has to do with accountability. In healthcare, it is called patient accountability. I have been out to a number of Web sites trying to see what the reaction might be to any system that asks a receiver of benefits to one day give back to the system if they ever come back from their financial crisis.

I was not looking for ways to move people off the welfare rolls or deny anybody access to life saving treatment. What I found was there are some very kind people on liberal blogs and there are some very practical and kind people on what would appear to be conservative blogs.

The kind bloggers clearly seem to believe that the government is actually an entity that has a life of its own and has its own resources. Most do not see government, as I do, which is like a club that has membership from the full population and all the members of the club provide the funding for the club. The members are motivated to support the club because there are things that one person does not do well, such as build roads, defend all the members from harm from another club, and other acts that are done better with group power.

The charter of the club says that the purpose is to promote the common good and does not give anybody in office an ability to confiscate dollars from the club treasury to give to any particular club member, or group of club members for any purpose. If a club member is down on their luck then the goodness of the human being would motivate club members individually, not collectively, to reach down and help those in need. That's the club I see as the government. Any confiscation of the treasury for any other purpose would not be permitted by the by-laws.

Yet, because most see government as something funded by the pot at the end of the rainbow and not by donations from club members, when asked if welfare people, when they are on their feet should give back to the people's treasury, on the liberal blog sites, many voted no. I hope that people reconsider that as there really should be no permanently free lunch in the US.

Sometimes it is good to drive arguments home ad absurdum. In this light, I present to you the bumper sticker of the year for 2009. See Figure 8-1.

Figure 8-1 Bumper Sticker Found on Internet, Summer 2009

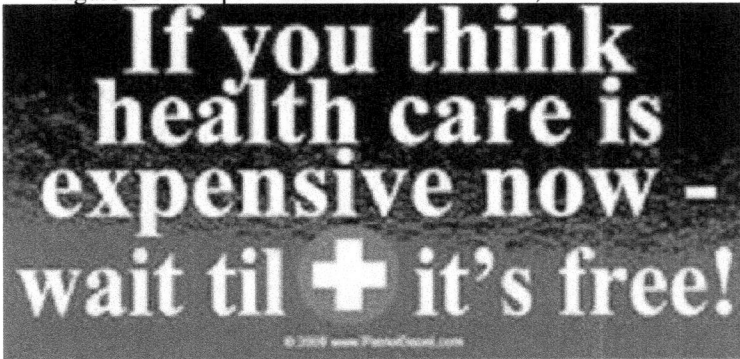

Chapter 9 Welfare Accountability

Free healthcare and income tax credits are welfare

In these troubling times, public welfare departments in the US are doing a fine business. They are without a doubt the fastest-growing departments in state and federal governments. Not only is the cost of actual assistance growing exponentially, but the appropriation needed to fund the permanent welfare state has grown substantially as well. Every day, the burden increases and with no payback scheduled-ever, the growth will be difficult to sustain.

Despite real reductions in caseloads during the 1980s, 1990s and 2000s, many state welfare bureaus did not reduce their cases and case workers. States should certainly stop this unwarranted growth in bureaucracy but then again, states have rights over and above those of the federal government.

Welfare legislation provides real financial penalties for state and county public welfare departments, as well for cash assistance programs. If, for example, a state public welfare department fails to meet a number of federal requirements, dollars may be withheld, or other penalties assessed to assure compliance. Since the federal government is like a great uncle to the states in providing money for welfare, the federal role cannot be minimized.

There are roughly 126 welfare programs overall that together comprise the single largest item in the federal budget — larger than Medicare, Social Security, or defense. Do you think 126 separate and distinct welfare programs is overkill?

There is s ton of money being given with no chance of getting any in return. We can't even send out no-cost electronic Christmas cards as a nation to those to whom the nation's welfare programs have rendered assistance. We have no idea who they are and how much they have received.

We give a lot of help to a lot of people, but we do not keep track of to whom we give the help because there is no requirement for repayment. I think we should keep track and we should be repaid. We do however, know the totals and they are growing astronomically.

The 2018 budget numbers are huge as shown below

View: people old function radical census programs altprog oldprog COFOG	Fed	Gov. Xfer	State	Local	Total
[+] Social Security	1,010.4	0.0	0.0	0.0	1,010.4
[+] Medicare (Net)	588.4	0.0	0.0	0.0	588.4
[–] Medicaid: *Start chart*	494.9	-403.7	617.8	6.0	715.0
[+] Vendor Payments (Welfare)	494.9	-403.7	617.8	6.0	715.0
[–] Other Welfare: *Start chart*	356.2	-118.1	106.4	94.7	439.2
[+] Family and children	268.1	-103.7	59.8	52.6	276.7
[+] Unemployment	37.5	-7.0	37.5	0.1	68.2
[+] Unemployment trust	0.0	0.0	0.0	0.0	0.0
[+] Workmens compensation	2.8	0.0	0.0	0.0	2.8
[+] Housing	47.9	-7.5	9.1	42.0	91.6
[+] Social exclusion n.e.c.	0.0	0.0	0.0	0.0	0.0
[+] R and D Social protection	0.0	0.0	0.0	0.0	0.0
[+] Social protection n.e.c.	0.0	0.0	0.0	0.0	0.0
[+] Gov. Employee Pensions (Net)	48.7	0.0	258.5	55.6	362.8
[+] Defense	885.9	0.0	0.9	0.0	886.8
[+] All Other Spending	709.9	-172.0	857.6	1,768.3	3,163.8
[+] Balance	-0.0	-0.0	9.7	-0.0	9.7
[+] Total Government Spending	4,094.5	-693.8	1,850.9	1,924.7	7,176.2
[+] Federal Deficit	440.2	0.0	0.0	0.0	440.2
[+] Gross Public Debt	21,093.3	0.0	1,183.8	1,914.2	24,191.3
[+] Agency/GSE Debt	9,260.7	0.0	0.0	0.0	9,260.7

To show how the numbers have grown in the last eight years, and to put the numbers in perspective, check this out. Not including Social Security and Medicare, Congress (the US government) directly allocated almost $717 billion in federal funds in 2010. Additionally, $210 billion was allocated in state funds ($927 billion total). This was all for means tested welfare programs in the United States, of which half was for medical care and roughly 40% for cash, food and housing assistance.

In 2016, the numbers skyrocketed to $871 billion in federal funds $(488 Billion Medicaid; $383 Billion for other welfare). State funds in 2016 amounted to just under $300 billion. Let's just say the total is $1000 Billion and that the Welfare part minus the medical (State and Federal), is $500 Billion. As you can see, they are up again in 2018.

What if over the last ten years, ½ of the welfare recipients got off welfare and became productive citizens with no dependence on the US for Medicaid or for welfare. That would be good. Suppose…just suppose that they began to pay back their welfare at 5% per year to make it simple.

That would mean that assuming a flow from prior years, there would be a $5% + 5% +5% +5% +5% +5% +5% +5% +5% +5% = a simple 50% of the funds paid back. 50% payback times 50% of the participants = 25% X 500 Billion = $125 Billion in payback. If we add Medicaid, we are at **$250 Billion**. It sure seems like this idea is at least worth of a feasibility test. Even if we do not get all the moneyback, $375 Billion is nothing to sneeze at.

Keeping track of healthcare expenditures would be more involved but as we head into Electronic Health Records (EHRs) as mandated by the government, expense tracking would simply be a by-product of the system.

Since the health part of the system would be designed to keep track of all kinds of small items amounts such as prescription drugs, lab tests, x-rays, and other medical procedures, adding the cost to the records would not be a challenge for any IT department.

Together, health and welfare, might amount to an individual having as many as 20 charges of various kinds in one month or an average of 240 per year. But, since it is mandated to track these for the federally mandated EHR system, the cost of the service should also be kept in the records.

To accomplish welfare repayments, the accountability systems would require less computer design work. The amount per transaction such as a monthly cash payment amounts or access card (Food Stamp) monthly refreshes would be substantially easier to process than a doctor's visit with multiple charges for different practice codes, or a prescription drug order.

Additionally, the entity paying in healthcare is a patient or Medicare paying a specific charge as it occurs. In welfare, it would be a government agency like the Welfare Department or Aid to Dependent children etc. A record of their monthly payments could be electronically forwarded to the big system in the Sky and coded as welfare—without all the work required of the healthcare charge tracking system.

If this system for welfare were implemented and we knew the details of all the handouts that have been ever given to any social security number, we could ask for something back. We could ask for say, 1%, or 5% at max for example, based on an ability to afford. This is often called means-testing when it is paid, and the same means test could be applied when the debt is paid off. Under no circumstances would the government be entitled to take more than 5% of earnings. Social Security income and Unemployment Compensation would be excluded from the payback formula.

This would have some startup bumps, but it would serve all taxpayers well. Americans would actually know where and how we are spending our welfare tax dollars. Additionally, we could get some money back into the system as citizens begin to do really well.

A New Beginning
Welfare to Work

Bill Clinton is not the most conservative politician in the world, for sure. Yet, even he saw a problem in 1996 and he devised a solution. Before the law was passed, with the help of Congress, more than 13 million people were receiving cash assistance from the government in 1996. In 2016, this number was down to 3 million.

Where there is a will there is a way. America is broke for sure and so, we need ways to pay for things more today than ever before. The Personal Accounting Record System (PAR) introduced can drastically help this along with a ton of new Donald Trump jobs.

"Simply put, welfare reform worked because we all worked together," Bill Clinton, who signed into law welfare reform, or the Personal Responsibility and Work Opportunity Reconciliation Act of 1996, wrote in an op-ed in The New York Times in 2006. Clinton had campaigned on a pledge to "end welfare as we know it" and today it is all too apparent that he succeeded.

In 2013, a person named Tiffy, an American, and a former college student, was concerned about welfare and whether or not people on welfare had to pay it back. Here is the question she asked from a blog on the Internet:

> Ok I have never been on it and don't know anyone who has. I did take out student loans, which I guess is a type of government assistance, and I have to pay those back. So, is welfare the same?
>
> Do people have to pay back what they received once they get a real job and are making enough money to cover all of their expenses? If not, why the hell not? I mean they are basically stealing money from taxpayers' right?
>
> If I take out a loan from the bank and don't repay it, they come either repo my car or foreclose on my home because that money belongs to the bank. So, if people refuse to repay welfare aren't they stealing from the tax payers and government? I understand some people need assistance, just like when people take out student loans, but why shouldn't they have to pay it back?

"Banned" offered a truthful guess that was right on the money:

> Depends on what you mean by 'welfare'. But most likely, no.

No is the right answer. No payments are required. It is not like a student loan, it is more like a huge Pell Grant. It is like a gift from the government just because you are you and you need the gift. Politicians like to give gifts, so they can be remembered as the gift-givers.

There are lots of ways those on the dole can get money from multiple government sources, 126 in all, and they are never required to pay any of it back even if they hit a $200 million lottery. Why is that?

Because there is no accountability for welfare. Those who give the money, the various agencies funded by taxpayers have decided it would be too much work to actually keep track of how much a given recipient has received.

Of course, trying to get something paid back is impossible unless we know what it is. We must account for it when it is given. As hard as it is to believe, the US government does not know to whom we give the benefits.

Don't you think we should know?

Do you trust the government to run such a system?

I do not.

I trust government with little.

Think of all the great systems that have been designed by the greatest corporations in the world. How often does one of them forget that you owe a dime. And, if they are charging interest, they never miss a dime. What if government were in charge. Let me just say that there would be special people, you know this is true, who would have payback exemptions. Our esteemed

Congress would want scholarships on loan repayments in their pocket, so they could make a big splash when they attended a constituent's wedding etc. Would it not be great for the Congressman to be able to give a loan forgiveness? Of course, it could only happen if the corrupt US government ran the program.

And, so, if I were in charge, I would without hesitation bring in a capable and honest company such as IBM. I would ask IBM to check out the best financial systems in the world. Chances are IBM built their software. Why not get IBM to modify the finest software in the world and through a consortium of doctors and others, build the best PAR System possible, borrowing and building as necessary.

Chapter 10 Summary & Conclusions

The helpless must be helped

Just so you know, our president, Donald Trump believes in the safety net for the American people. So, do I. President Trump also believes in accountability. He is a good man. He believes that we should help helpless people, but he also believes that government programs should not make people helpless.

Unlike many in the former administration such as VP Biden, who has a dismal charity record, Donald Trump believes that he and other wealthy Americans such as Mr. Biden and Mr. Obama and Hillary Clinton and Mitt Romney should relinquish their Social Security benefits and donate them back to the country. President Trump as many know, takes no salary. He is doing a great job for America because he loves America.

He knows that widespread fraud exists in the Medicare, disability insurance, and food stamp programs. Trump supported Bill Clinton's 1996 Welfare Reform Act's work requirement.

Nobody really wants to be lectured about anything. Nobody wants to be put down when they are already down. Nobody wants the safety net that they always believed was between them and the end to be weakened or destroyed. Nobody wants what is theirs to be taken away so that somebody else can have it—no matter how deserving the other may be.

Mostly everybody believes that when you can provide for yourself, you should provide for yourself. Mostly everybody believes that anybody who chooses not to work for theirs should not be able to take yours forcibly. If you choose to give up your holdings to help another, your gain will be in heaven.

The whole idea of welfare accountability, as put forth in this book, is so that those in need are helped as much as they need but no more. If it is a health issue, those needing care should get the care.

Everybody who needs help and cannot provide for themselves should get the help they need to come through their period of distress. That's the American way. Nobody suggests that anybody should ever ignore symptoms & problems just because it would cost the state less if they ignored their issues.

I do fear that this new state, this highly socialistic state, that does not care about individuals per se, would be quite happy if many of us would choose to wither and /or die rather than collect our social security checks and spend our Medicare dollars on our health. That is not the theme of this book, but it is seems to be the deal of the new bureaucracy of a government emerging from what was an Obamacare driven government.

For eight years, with death panels in the offing, if you had a weakness that would have cost Obama some cash, the subtle message in Obamacare's death panels was: *why not just end it?* It still is. The Republicans never said the death panels would be repealed. That is another reason why many seniors are already enjoying the Trump presidency. Their lives have already been extended without getting the panel's permission.

The bureaucrats are chomping at the bit to be freed to regulate us in ways that benefits society rather than we as individuals. This has been the calling card of Dr. Ezekiel Emanuel who was, of course, a major Obama Health Advisor and major advocate of healthcare rationing, with less concern for seniors than other Americans. Emanuel is well published regarding his suggested system of healthcare rationing based on what he calls the "complete lives system." President Trump must undue Emanuel's work.

The complete lives system simply "discriminates against older people" in that it values how much time a 60-year old theoretically has left on earth as a major determinant compared to say, a ten-year old. No wonder why 60-year-olds can purchase liquor and ten-year-olds cannot.

If there were a lot of ten-year-olds in line at the doctors' offices, sixty-year-olds would (according to Emanuel's ideas) be sent home, without the need to pack ever again. But, according to Obama when he was president, Bayer quality aspirins would always be available for old farts even if their blood needed no thinning.

I like the idea that healthcare, to an extent, is either unlimited or self-limiting and those who can pay get it and those that cannot pay are at the mercy of those that can pay. Work should bring with it some benefits. Whether welfare or healthcare, if government gives it for free, somebody, aka, the taxpayers have paid for it.

How about, when people are fully able to pay back what they got for "free," the government sends them a friendly little note and watch the payback checks roll-in. Our country is bankrupt, so we could sure use all the help we can get.

In essence, instead of a gift, government checks that are not part of Unemployment Compensation or Medicare or Social Security will in the future be looked at as loans. If the recipient of the loan is never in a position to pay back any of the loan, so be it. It is no worse than today. But, if the recipient is in different circumstances, I would expect that they would be happy to pay back small amounts to the government. Nobody will go broke paying back a little at a time if they can.

In the PAR plan, the notion is brought forth that all who have received help can pay something back – even if just one percent, since the system would automatically, in essence, write a loan for all welfare receipts and for EMTALA care or for Medicaid assistance. This would be like insurance for somebody who cannot pay right away for services and "stuff" that is consumed.

I believe that if we train people to be slothful, we harvest sloths and non-productive people. Therefore, I would make sure that anybody on any cash form of welfare at a minimum, would have two to five dollars per welfare payment taken out and put back into the PAR fund as a payment. It is good to get people accustomed to paying for things. When they are more capable, they can request the amount be increased if they choose.

I do worry about the subtleties and the coldness of an administration that sets artificial maximums for colonoscopies and other medical procedures and they are willing to permit women to die as individuals for the greater cost-saving of society.

Fox news Sunday addressed rationing the day after the Senate approved debate on the original Obamacare bill. It was during a week in which the bureaucrats let loose with their limiting recommendations on Mammograms and perhaps on Pap tests.

The news for those listening was the new idea (back then) that the idea of women dying is now okay because it "costs too much" for society to find out which 40-year olds are going to get cancer. Hmmm!

On Fox, the Segment 2 Guest was Dr. Bernadine Healy, U.S. News & World Report's Health Editor & Former Director of the National Institutes of Health (NIH). She is an impressive person and she minced no words calling this a bureaucratic bumble of Obamacare rationing at its finest. She acknowledged that the bureaucrats do understand that their guidelines will mean that more women will die of breast cancer, but she suggests that is okay in the minds of the bureaucrats because dollars will be saved.

On the same show, the late Arlen Specter talked about "outsourcing" the downgrading of Medicare by $500 billion and as much as $700 Billion to assure the cuts are made. His case was to position the Congress, so it could then pull a Pontius Pilate on its implementation and blame it on the guys they hire. Where is the last truthful man?

I believe in individualism. I believe that every member of society should fight as hard as they can so that every other member of society should be kept well. I do not believe healthcare is an inalienable right, but I do believe it is a duty of all to assure that no one goes without proper treatment. For the receiver of treatment, while receiving, nobody collects – just like EMTALA, but when well, the cost of the service is due.

I do not think that the mythical collectivism of society would be enhanced while we knowingly make decisions about the type of people who are permitted to survive in the future. An initiative that would allow the bureaucrats to become grim reapers is an absolute abomination and completely avoidable.

Think of the notion of the PAR as a loan and ask yourself if this cannot expand the ability of our system to pay for healthcare. Think about the individual and the individual's three people within—me, myself, and I, as being held accountable as the number one reason why any of us get to be healthy. It is time for Healthcare and Welfare Accountability.

I trust that the smart people in America will read books like this and some others and that others will listen to people like Michael Savage so that we do not let the Marxists doom us to an early grave simply because we have had a cold for more than two weeks or we have not eaten in two-weeks. Nobody should die from neglect in America.

Don't forget how nice it will be when everybody can contribute to their own healthcare, either while they are on their feet or off. Personal accountability should make everybody feel lots better.

One Last Anecdote

Once there was a family that had two sons. One son was very tuned in and very smart and he worked hard to make sure that the family did well. The other son was very smart, but he used his smarts to be lazy and he felt like since he was given life by his parents, they should make sure he was always okay.

The industrious son was always told that his brother needed special care, but, deep down he knew they were equal in need but not will. As the sons got older, the parents, approaching the end of their lives, began to give them both part of their savings in equal proportions.

The industrious son was never heralded for his good works. Yet, much of the parent's saving had come because of the industriousness of this son who had worked hard every day. As this son observed equal shares given to his brother, who chose not to work, he was confused about what to do. So, he decided that he too would take life easy and disbursements began to exceed resources and income. Eventually, the family fell out of prosperity and ... well, maybe it did not have to end this way.

When things are not fair, very often individuals change their behavior to even up the score. If work has no payoff, why work?

We are all accountable and in order to ensure continued prosperity we must all be held accountable for our actions and our debts. Our nation was built on the blood, sweat and tears of a generation that equated personal accountability with the very freedom that we have enjoyed for generations henceforth. It's not too late to unite as individuals, to fight for our own right to have a role in our own welfare and healthcare process and to assure accountability for all welfare checks and medical assistance.

Now, I am going to show off by signing off this book with a great German phrase:

Gesundheit!

Other books by Brian Kelly: (<small>amazon.com, and Kindle</small>)

Wipe Out Student Debt Now! Watch the economic boom by one smart stimulus act.
Boost Social Security Now! Hey Buddy Can You Spare a Dime?
The Birth of American Football. From the first college game in 1869 to the last Super Bowl
Obamacare: A One-Line Repeal Congress must get this done.
A Wilkes-Barre Christmas Story A wonderful town makes Christmas all the better
A Boy, A Bike, A Train, and a Christmas Miracle A Christmas story that will melt your heart
Pay-to-Go America-First Immigration Fix
Legalizing Illegal Aliens Via Resident Visas Americans-first plan saves $Trillions. Learn how!
60 Million Illegal Aliens in America!!! A simple, America-first solution.
The Bill of Rights By Founder James Madison Refresh *your knowledge of the specific rights for all*
Great Players in Army Football Great Army Football played by great players..
Great Coaches in Army Football Army's coaches are all great.
Great Moments in Army Football Army Football at its best.
Great Moments in Florida Gators Football Gators Football from the start. This is the book.
Great Moments in Clemson Football CU Football at its best. This is the book.
Great Moments in Florida Gators Football Gators Football from the start. This is the book.
The Constitution Companion. A Guide to Reading and Comprehending the Constitution
The Constitution by Hamilton, Jefferson, & Madison – Big type and in English
PATERNO: The Dark Days After Win # 409. Sky began to fall within days of win # 409.
JoePa 409 Victories: Say No More! Winningest Division I-A football coach ever
American College Football: The Beginning From before day one football was played.
Great Coaches in Alabama Football Challenging the coaches of every other program!
Great Coaches in Penn State Football the Best Coaches in PSU's football program
Great Players in Penn State Football The best players in PSU's football program
Great Players in Notre Dame Football The best players in ND's football program
Great Coaches in Notre Dame Football The best coaches in any football program
Great Players in Alabama Football from Quarterbacks to offensive Linemen Greats!
Great Moments in Alabama Football AU Football from the start. This is the book.
Great Moments in Penn State Football PSU Football, start--games, coaches, players,
Great Moments in Notre Dame Football ND Football, start, games, coaches, players
Cross Country With the Parents A great trip from East Coast to West with the kids
Seniors, Social Security & the Minimum Wage. Things seniors need to know.
How to Write Your First Book and Publish It with CreateSpace
The US Immigration Fix--It's all in here. Finally, an answer.
I had a Dream IBM Could be #1 Again The title is self-explanatory
WineDiets.Com Presents The Wine Diet Learn how to lose weight while having fun.
Wilkes-Barre, PA; Return to Glory Wilkes-Barre City's return to glory
Geoffrey Parsons' Epoch... The Land of Fair Play Better than the original.
The Bill of Rights 4 Dummmies! This is the best book to learn about your rights.
Sol Bloom's Epoch ...Story of the Constitution The best book to learn the Constitution
America 4 Dummmies! All Americans should read to learn about this great country.
The Electoral College 4 Dummmies! How does it really work?
The All-Everything Machine Story about IBM's finest computer server.
ThankYou IBM! This book explains how IBM was beaten in the computer marketplace by neophytes

Brian has written 135 books in total. Other books can be found at amazon.com/author/brianwkelly